························

THOUGHTS AND THINGS

· · · · · · · · · · · · ·

LEO BERSANI

Thoughts and Things

THE

UNIVERSITY OF

CHICAGO PRESS

CHICAGO AND

LONDON

Leo Bersani is
professor emeritus
of French at the
University of
California, Berkeley.
He is the author of
numerous books,
including *Is the
Rectum a Grave?"
and Other Essays*,
published by
the University of
Chicago Press.

The University of Chicago Press, Chicago 60637

The University of Chicago Press, Ltd., London

24 23 22 21 20 19 18 17 16 15   1 2 3 4 5

ISBN-13: 978-0-226-20605-9   (cloth)

ISBN-13: 978-0-226-20619-6   (e-book)

DOI: 10.7208/chicago/9780226206196.001.0001

Library of Congress Cataloging-in-Publication Data

Bersani, Leo, author.

Thoughts and Things / Leo Bersani.

    pages   cm

Includes index.

ISBN 978-0-226-20605-9 (cloth : alk. paper) —

ISBN 978-0-226-20619-6 (e-book) 1. Ontology.

2. Thought and thinking. 3. Self. I. Title.

BD331.B475 2015

110—dc23   2014019942

CONTENTS

AGAINST PREFACES?

A preface frequently saves us from the labor of reading the book it introduces. Perhaps not exactly from reading the book (although a really "good" preface can even do that), but from the work, what can be the pain of reading. Because a preface is customarily written after the rest of the book has been completed, it has a unique relation to the textual body for which it prepares us. It knows what we are letting ourselves in for, and it genially (if for the most part laboriously) cushions the shock.

This is the function assigned to prefaces by those institutions most fully and most proudly committed to what is revered as the life of the mind. Thus thousands of Ph.D. candidates are advised (directed) to prepare, as their final piece of work in the doctoral process, a short discussion of what their dissertation is about. (Would that students could afford the luxury of an exasperated refusal to heed that request!—a luxury enjoyed and suffered by Jerzy, the director of the film being made within Jean-Luc Godard's film *Passion,* through whom Godard warns us not to hound him about the sense of this film "about" the making of a film.)

We have all experienced the dreary relief of knowing in advance what awaits us in chapter 1, then in chapter 2, and so on. At the extreme limit of this advance knowledge of a text, the reader can hardly be blamed for expecting little more from the chapters themselves than multiple repetitions and inevitable illustrations of the arguments already laid out in the preface. From this perspective, a preface allows us to digest what it is presumably inviting us to taste. An after posing as a before, the "I will show" of our prefaces is a promissory transformation of "I have done."

Is the preface as I have just described it a genre unto itself? Not exactly: if it belongs to a category of writing practiced elsewhere, it is that of the notoriously tedious book report by which—at least in the secondary schools of yesteryear (that is, during my high school years)—students were expected to prove that they had read the assigned texts. The book report was not invented as an early experience in critical writing; rather, it was meant to be an accurate summary, a confirmation that the student had both done the homework and "gotten it right." Happily, a large number of author-written prefaces fail to pass this test, to fulfill the function of smoothing the path for desired readers, of guaranteeing that their reading experience will not be plagued by questions, objections, and failures to understand.

As the wise editor surely knows, it is more difficult to get oneself right than to think we understand somebody else. In those long-past book reports, we knew the other only as one written volume. In the case of a text I myself have written, how can I not be aware of at least some of the smothered objections I had in the process of writing, as well as of what has been eliminated in heavily (and perhaps unfortunately) revised passages—and even of other things I've written that may be inconsistent with, or contradict, the text I'm introducing? My long history as (to invoke Descartes) both a thinking and a writing thing risks making obscure my attempted summary of one moment of that history. Will I be making myself more accessible through this condensed recapitulation of what I have just written, or will I unintentionally be revealing a certain ignorance of what I was doing in the text I'm trying to present, and thereby providing the outline for another—revised, corrected—text not yet written? In short, am I increasing the readability of the work already written, or am I running the risk—however earnestly I have set out to do the opposite—of making not only the textual body but also the introduction to it problematic, even somewhat unreadable?

Of course, good editors know all this, and in asking their writers to provide their texts with prefaces, they may (we can never know how complicated they are) secretly be inviting them to make their books more interestingly opaque rather than more boringly transparent. For example, in agreeing to add a conventional preface to *Thoughts and Things,* I suppose I would say that all the essays in this book—most of which were not written as part of a single book project—treat the question of connectedness: of how the human subject connects or fails to connect to other human subjects and to the nonhuman world.

As part of my effort to convince readers that the different parts of my work do belong together in a single book, I might suggest that they begin by reading chapter 3, where the relational motif is most fully elaborated conceptually. My argument there is that a major current in Western thought has emphasized the disjunction between the self and the world. A Cartesian assumption of the ontological gap separating *res cogitans* from *res extensa* may account for what both Michel Foucault and Richard Rorty, in different contexts, have emphasized as the prioritizing of knowledge in modern thought as the dominant relational mode of the human subject's being-in-the-world. Thinkers as different as Descartes, Freud, and Proust have accustomed us to thinking of our connection to otherness in terms of epistemological appropriation and possession.

Chapter 3 also underlines an important similarity between Cartesianism and psychoanalysis. Freud's version of Descartes's dualism is an argument about the external world's foreignness to the human subject. Descartes subdues otherness through knowledge; the Freudian subject works to reduce the always potentially hostile otherness of the external world through such familiar psychic operations as incorporation and projection. The question I ask is why it has been so easy to emphasize the differential nature of otherness—as if we had perversely worked to subordinate the possibilities of exchange with otherness (a correspondence with or belonging to what is other) to a conflictive, often violent relation to difference. Chapter 3 ends with a brief invocation of philosophers (from Spinoza to Merleau-Ponty) who, within what Foucault thought of as the hegemony of Cartesian thought in modern Western culture, have elaborated the modes of our connectedness to external reality, of a productively relational rather than intrinsically oppositional presence in the world.

In saying all this, I am perhaps letting myself be carried away by something like the essence of The Preface, an essence whose power I set out to resist. However, having reduced myself to a principal idea or theme, I have come to see how these essays, not having originally been written as chapters of single book, are in fact connected. And not just because they are all about connectedness: they have a complex structural connectedness that is analogous to but richer than their thematic connections. The first two chapters, most notably, are actually domesticated by the ideas developed (you might say thematized) in the chapter that follows them. The great power of Claire Denis's film *Beau travail* (discussed in chapter 1) is that it existentializes not only the oppositional violence that both connects and tears apart a human subject and the world he or she inhabits, but also a certain at-homeness in the world that exists alongside that violence. *Alongside* is crucial: the sociality beautifully embodied in the Legionnaires is not exactly resistant to the violence embodied in their superior, Galoup. It is, interestingly, juxtaposed with it, as if it could be an alternative to Galoup only if it implicitly recognized its inability to do away with his world of conflict. There may be a mode of sociality that is neither complicitous nor oppositional in its relation to intractable violence, a sociality that acknowledges a violence to which, however, it is constitutively devoid of any relation.

The removal from an oppressive mode of connectedness is even more radically exemplified in the works I discuss in chapter 2. In Jean Genet's *Our Lady of the Flowers,* Divine not only escapes from her biological maleness into her self-fashioned identity as Pigalle's most fabulous transvestite whore. Even that identity wavers at moments when a distraught Divine finds herself floating in an undefined, ungendered territory between male and female. And for Carol in Todd Haynes's film *Safe,* a sensitivity to toxic chemicals in the environment grows into what seems like an allergy to the universe itself. By the end of the film, she has almost become no one. Through what appears to be an involuntary but unqualified negativity, she has simply disappeared from any psychic or social identity.

These preludes to the thematic center of *Thoughts and Things* are not exactly—are not exact—exemplifications of the next chapter's philosophical argument. In agreeing to provide a prefatory intelligibility to the essays collected in this book (to make them readable before they are read), I may have failed to do that in a way that makes the collection more interesting and, strangely, more readable in unexpected ways. The positing of an irreducible gap of being between the human subject and the world is assumed rather than stated in *Beau travail, Our Lady of the Flowers,* and *Safe.* It is assumed by the factitious nature of the connections (familial, gendered, and social) proposed in these works. The validity of the argument made in chapter 3 is not necessarily confirmed by a subjective awareness of that gap. Rather, it can be obliquely attested to by the relational identities imposed on the subject.

In chapter 2 I invoke Pierre Bourdieu's invaluable analyses of how a culture legitimates or delegitimates psychic and social identities and positions. Identitarian and relational authorizations fill the gap of being between the subject and the world (at the same time that they mask the oneness that, I will be arguing in chapters 4 and 5, is intrinsic to our being in and with the world). Attempted escapes from the cultural conferring of legitimacy and nonlegitimacy can bring the subject back to an aloneness that is different from the conquering autonomy toward which the Cartesian subject aspires, and that may be the precondition for new points of entry into a hospitable otherness to which we have always (if unknowingly) belonged. Thus, while I think that the argument made in chapter 3 has historical and philosophical value, my reluctant recognition of the necessity of a preface has led me to a new appreciation of a superficially more modest movement of ideas in the earlier chapters, compared to an instructive and yet somewhat flashy thematizing of that movement. To summarize this in Hegelian terms, I'm tempted to affirm the ontological superiority of determinateness over the notion embodied in (and, ultimately, superseded by) the determinate.

Having said all this, I see no need to provide a complete guide to chapters 4 and 5, although they are probably the most intellectually dense of all the essays in *Thoughts and Things*. Recognition of the oneness of being—of our intrinsic connectedness to the otherness at once external and, from a psychoanalytic perspective, internal to us—requires, it seems to me, a modification of our fundamental terms of thought. With the opposition between *res cogitans* and *res externa*, Descartes initiates us to a regime of divided being. Psychoanalysis internalizes this regime with its concept of a divided self. Another version of the world's differential otherness is repeated within the subject as the unconscious, an "area" of the mind with both a content and a syntax alien to the usual content and syntax of conscious thinking.

In chapter 4, I attempt to formulate the relational terms, the syntax, of an undivided mind, one in which present consciousness always includes both past thought and unconscious thought. The latter are not separate, distinct entities; they are recategorized as a virtual present within a vast psychic reality that is always present. This is the subjective corollary of a oneness of being in which the subject never ceases to correspond with, and to, the world. In chapter 5, I suggest that contemporary cosmological theory invites us to think of ourselves as extending now into a cosmic past. Our bodies contain atoms from stars that exploded millions of years ago. *Res cogitans* and *res extensa* are united in the oneness of cosmic being.

Having dutifully obeyed the injunction to say what I think I have done in the following chapters, and without wishing to return to my (understandably irritating) fussiness about the nature of The Preface itself, I'm nonetheless uncertain about whether or not these few pages will have made my readers more intellectually relaxed as they enter into those chapters. It may not be helpful for me to confess that I am myself stymied by chapter 6. And this is not because it is more difficult than the other chapters, but rather because I'm not sure why I have placed it at the end of the book. I set out in *Thoughts and Things* to argue for psychic and cosmic connectedness, a project that concludes grandly in chapter 5 by extending our material, embodied present to the origins of the universe. The final chapter, "Being and Notness," is an anomaly in that it is a close study of an almost unqualified failure to connect.

The narrator's father in Pierre Bergounioux's brilliant, and very peculiar, short novel *La Casse,* having never known his own father, is unable to acknowledge his son's existence. His project, recognized with despair by his loving son, is to reduce the latter to notness. Not only does the son (the work's narrator) find that Descartes's optimism about all human subjects participating, as "thinking things," in a universal community of thought is of no use in bringing his father to recognize their oneness. There is also the implicit assumption that it is only through the father—through his love and his law—that we can enter the human community, a psychoanalytic assumption questioned by the Claire Denis film discussed in chapter 1.

So why conclude on this somber note—unless it testifies to my psychoanalytically inspired conviction, which I have elaborated elsewhere, about an intractable destructiveness intrinsic to being human, a destructiveness always ready to shatter the oneness of being, which it thereby mocks as a cosmic illusion. It has perhaps been useful, I now realize, to qualify my utopic tendencies by giving the last word to an uncompromising negativity.

In writing what began as an ill-humored introduction to *Thoughts and Things,* I have, then, discovered what I probably should already have known. I have become a little strange to myself, and in so doing I have had the opportunity to become my first critical reader. Thanks to this preface, the readers of these essays should have the added profit of testing what I have been saying about them instead of merely being subjected to a verbose elaboration of central ideas summarized in a few introductory pages. I have varying degrees of distance from the chapters of this book. I am, however, sufficiently separated from all of them to ensure a frictional rather than simply tautological relation of this preliminary piece to the essays it purports to introduce. I might, nonetheless, have wished for more time to have elapsed between the two, having recently experienced the enlivening effect of a considerable period of time having passed between a new preface and a book published many years ago.

On the occasion of the reissuing of my first book, a 1965 study of Proust titled *Marcel Proust: The Fictions of Life and of Art,* I was, predictably, asked to provide a new preface to this, for me, old work. Sufficiently old so that I could begin the preface with the confession of an estrangement between two moments in the history of my writing self: "The author of this book is remotely familiar to me." At the distance of nearly half a century, I think I was able to present my much earlier critical self with a laudable mixture of generosity (toward the first of my many confrontations with Proust's massive work) and reserve (toward arguments I would still make, but recategorized within, I would hope, an enriched critical apparatus). In the present instance, it strikes me that the blend of sameness and difference between the essays themselves and what I have just written, pleasurably if reluctantly, about them aligns me with those who have not yet read the essays. As my first reader, I have found a strangeness in my work not entirely unlike the disorienting but productive difference ideally encountered by someone reading a text for the first time. I hope not to have succeeded in having my preface coincide exactly with the essays that follow it (thereby displaying the tedious confidence of someone certain of being at one with himself). Not being entirely sure of what I have done, I have become not the reader's friendly but superior facilitator, but rather an anticipatory (if obviously more privileged) version of all the first-time readers of this text. In already participating in the critical distance of those readers, I have enacted a connectedness that, to make it all as starkly simple as possible, is the subject of this book.

1 ·

FATHER KNOWS BEST

At the beginning of our discussion of Alain Resnais's films in *Arts of Impoverishment,* Ulysse Dutoit and I ask: "Is there a nonsadistic type of movement? Would we go toward the world if we were not motivated by destructive impulses?" These questions seemed to us an appropriate response to Freud's assumption of a fundamental, ineradicable antagonism between the human subject and the world. Toward the end of the 1915 essay "Instincts and Their Vicissitudes," Freud claims: "At the very beginning, it seems, the external world, objects, and what is hated are identical." The infantile ego, we went on in our summary of Freud's argument, "must defend itself against the external stimuli by which it is bombarded; hatred is at first a self-preservative reflex." The unobjectionable nature of this claim becomes problematic when Freud repeats it without either the tentative qualification of "it seems" or the temporal specifying of its relevance. The repudiation of the world—of all the difference that threatens the ego's stability (indeed its very constitution as a distinct identity)—is, it turns out, by no means limited to infancy. "As an expression of the unpleasure evoked by objects," Freud goes on, "hate always remains in an intimate relation with the self-preservative instincts."

This is the psychoanalytic formulation of the structural relation generally recognized as central to the Western notion of the bond between mind and the world, the relation of subjects to objects. The originality of psychoanalysis in this history is its emphasis on the

This chapter was previously published as "Father Knows Best" in *Raritan* 29, no. 4 (Spring 2010).

inherently violent nature of the subject-object relation. It is no longer a question of determining how mind, thought, or reason can know the world (can reach that truth succinctly described by Aquinas as "adequation of the intellect and the thing"), or of demonstrating the impossibility of any such equivalence (and arguing instead, as Kant does in the *Critique of Pure Reason*, against the mistake of taking the formal conditions of thinking, conditions that determine objects, for the cognition of things in themselves). The psychoanalytic shift of emphasis in this history does not, however, question the assumption of a difference of being between the subject and the world. Indeed, it gives an affective emphasis to that assumption. The subject-object dualism in the history of philosophy has been the generally unquestioned and justificatory basis for the primordial importance of epistemology in philosophical investigations. It has dictated the terms that frame discussion of the subject's presence in the world. That discussion, as Richard Rorty pointed out several years ago, has, especially since Locke and Descartes, been heavily biased—a bias analyzed by Foucault as the elevation of knowledge over what he calls "care of the self," or spirituality, in post-Cartesian constructs of subjectivity.

By its very insistence on the techniques the subject uses to erase the gap separating it from the world of human and nonhuman objects—techniques of incorporation, identification, and projection—psychoanalysis insists on the affective pressures that motivate supposedly disinterested pursuits of knowledge. Once the object is seen not only as unknown but as threateningly unknown (or, to extend Jean Laplanche's use of the term, once the entire world is received as an enigmatic signifier resisting the will to know and the skills of knowing), the epistemological passion must be reformulated as the passion to appropriate the object and, at the limit, to destroy difference itself. The question of whether knowledge is possible eludes the assumptions that are its condition of possibility: first, that knowing or not knowing defines our primary relation to the world, and, second, that differences of being can be overcome by the mastery of difference, by what Freud, in "Instincts and Their Vicissitudes," curiously calls a nonsexual sadism.

It is perhaps this sadism that the early Jacques Lacan reformulates as the aggressiveness inherent in the relational imaginary. Because, he writes in his seminar on the psychoses, a foreign image—the image of the other misapprehended as the reality of a fragmented subject—institutes the function of psychic unification, the equilibrium with the other in the imaginary register will remain unstable. The other is always on the point of readopting his original place of mastery. The conflictual instability traceable, in Lacan, to the misrecognition inherent in the mirror stage specifies, as a stage of ego development, the Freudian antagonism between the self and the world. Both accounts, however, rely on a prior structural assumption of essential difference between the subject and the world.

An intersubjectivity grounded in the subject-object dualism is perhaps inevitably condemned (however its etiology may be understood) to a paranoid relationality. If otherness is reduced to difference, the hatred of the world that Freud speaks of— which we might rephrase as a paranoid suspicion of the world's difference—is, as he suggests, the affective basis of a logically coherent strategy of defense. The desire to know the other is inseparable from the need to master the other. The desire for mastery motivates the desire to know, and knowledge is the precondition of mastery. But what does it mean to know another human subject? As Foucault has emphasized, in the modern period to know the other is to know the other's desire. The most distinctive aspect of the other's individuality is how and what he or she desires. The most powerful pre-Freudian version of this view of intersubjectivity as a struggle to possess the other's desire is the Hegelian master-slave dialectic, a process that assumes, as Alexandre Kojève puts it in his lectures on Hegel's *Phenomenology*, that "desire is human only if the one desires, not the body, but the Desire of the other. Indeed, the human being is formed only in terms of a

Desire directed toward another Desire, that is—finally—in terms of a desire for 'recognition.'"

This struggle between defensive fortresses of individualizing desires has been benignly and naively reformulated as the basis of the analytic cure: the analyst's "possession" of the analysand's desires becomes the gift the former gives to the latter, the key to a liberating self-knowledge. Psychoanalysis shifts the investigative emphasis from the nature and conditions of knowledge, or from the desire to know, to the desire to know desire. Even more: the success of analytic knowledge depends on the displacement of the knowing subject from the analyst to the analysand. In this shift within the subject-object relation, the dualism is re-created *within* the subject as subject-mind and object-mind.

The divided self—essential to the psychoanalytic notion of subjectivity—has perhaps always been the psychic ground supporting the subject-object dualism in notions of the relation between the self and the world. The world seen as differential otherness is the displaced repetition (and misrecognition) of the subject's perception of a differential otherness within himself. Proust, who has given us the most complete representation of what we might call the psychoanalytic subject, analyzes Marcel's jealousy of Albertine in exactly these terms. Once his obsessive jealousy—which in Proust always means the obsessive need to penetrate the other's desires—has been unleashed by Albertine's revelation of her friendship with the lesbian Mlle. Vinteuil, Marcel makes her a virtual prisoner in his parents' apartment while explicitly recognizing that the Albertine who has suddenly become the object of his doomed need to know is actually not outside of him but within him. What Marcel calls the "inconceivable truth" of Albertine's desires is a projection of the inconceivability of Marcel's desires. Albertine's consciousness is a screen for the otherness hidden within Marcel's consciousness. "All jealousy," the narrator writes, "is self-jealousy."

What are the alternatives to a relationality guided by an ideology of difference, one in which the ontological premise of a subject-object dualism gives primacy to the quest for knowledge in the subject's relation both to himself and to the world? Ulysse Dutoit and I have been studying for several years, principally in the visual arts, models for an aesthetic ethic of correspondences between the self and the world, a community of being in which the recognition of various degrees and modes of similitude is itself a sensually appealing deconstruction of the prestige of knowledge. And in *Intimacies*, our recently published book, Adam Phillips and I argue that "psychoanalysis has misled us into believing, in its quest for narrative life-stories, that knowledge of oneself and others is conducive to intimacy, [and] that intimacy is by definition personal intimacy." Without attempting to write a history of the conception and representation of intimacy in Western culture, we use certain political, aesthetic, and philosophical texts with the intention of reconceptualizing psychoanalytic notions of intimacy—more specifically, to elaborate a concept of impersonal intimacy and even impersonal narcissism as a viable alternative to what seems to us the limiting and harmful assumption that intimacy necessarily includes, indeed may depend on, a knowledge of the other's personal psychology.

It has seemed to me that at least as persuasively as most philosophical arguments, certain films have reflected cinematically on the issues just raised. More particularly, I've been interested in films that seem to be testing definitions and conditions of intimacy and, in so doing, have proposed new or at least unfamiliar relational configurations. The film I will discuss here addresses directly the question I raised earlier: Is there a nonsadistic type of movement? Claire Denis's remarkable 1999 work, *Beau travail* (released only in 2000), focuses on a group of Foreign Legionnaires stationed in Djibouti, where the film was made. It was commissioned by the French film company Arte for its series *Terres étrangères* (Foreign Lands).

The Legionnaires of *Beau travail* are professional actors (the men stationed at the Djibouti Foreign Legion outpost received Denis and her crew with hostility), and the visual, pseudodocumentary account of their lives is very much an aesthetic and, more specifically, a choreographic construction. The African setting is nonetheless a fitting topographical metaphor for what Denis thought of as the center of her film: being a foreigner to one's own life. The reality that historically supports Denis's fable of foreignness is that of the Legion itself, created under Louis-Philippe in 1831 and consisting of recruits from several countries (only about a quarter of Legionnaires have been French). The men in the Legion, while under French authority, are the off-spring of no single state. The Legion is an international collection of ethnically orphaned men, many of them displaced foreign nationals with a past from which the Legion allows them to escape, who as Legionnaires have no parental community outside the nearly autonomous, we might even say unengendered, collectivity to which they are expected to have a fierce loyalty. Their rallying cry is *Legio patria nostra*: The Legion [not France] is our homeland. The communitarianism of the Foreign Legion is entirely self-created; the Legion constitutes its own paternity.

It is within this unique human formation that belongs nowhere and is expected to be ready to move anywhere that Denis tests the identities—realized, potential, erased identities—produced by different kinds of movement. The film's fundamental structure is a juxtaposition of two contrasting types of mobility. In addition to the choreographic mobility to which I will return, there is the narrative movement of the plot, a plot fairly close to yet also significantly different from the drama of Melville's *Billy Budd*. The new, beautiful Legionnaire Sentain is singled out by Galoup, the men's master sergeant, as bringing a discordant note to the group, as somehow not being an authentic Legionnaire. But except for the sense we may have of something exceptionally quiet or private about Sentain, of an occasionally perceptible withdrawal from the lively group spirit of his fellow Legionnaires, Sentain hardly stands out as someone radically different from the others in the way that the inarticulate, stuttering Billy Budd, called the Handsome Sailor, is recognized, affectionately and protectively, by his comrades as bringing a childlike innocence to the isolated sea-borne society of the *Bellipotent*. Galoup searches for and finally finds a pretext to punish Sentain (whom Galoup has provoked into striking him) by leaving him alone in the desert with nothing but a compass, deliberately damaged by Galoup, to guide him back to the Legion encampment. Galoup is told by Forestier, his commander (called in French *le chef de corps*), that having dishonored himself by his treachery against Sentain, he can no longer be part of the Legion, and Galoup returns to civilian life in Marseille.

The filmic account of these events is not entirely linear. There are shots of the disgraced Galoup in Marseille at the beginning of *Beau travail*. Scenes of his returning to France and of his daily life in Marseille alternate with the Djibouti narrative, as does what Denis has called the "parallel text" of Galoup's voice-over recital of passages from his diary, almost all of it written after his return to Marseille. The filmic narrative, at once linear and retrospective, is thus partially detemporalized; it has the remoteness of events already settled in the completeness of an indefinitely repeatable, potentially mythic story. The quality of something that has already taken place (and that may always be taking place) does not immobilize the drama; yet it does give to the narrative movement of that drama the inexorable quality of a psychic story that doesn't need time to unfold, that can't be affected or stopped by time, that has an imaginary and, as a consequence, a historically invulnerable totality.

That story is a family story, the inherently violent narrative not, in this version of familial violence, of the son's rivalry with the father for the mother's love, but of the less familiar fratricidal rivalry for the father's love. This is not, I might note, the story of *Billy Budd*. Melville renounces any attempt to explain psychologically the hatred that Billy's beauty and innocence arouse in Claggart. "Apprehending the good [in Billy]," he writes, but powerless to embrace it, Claggart is driven to destroy the embodiment of that good by "the elemental evil in him." Though he is at first "moved against Billy" by the latter's "significant personal beauty," Claggart's envy, Melville insists, "struck deeper." It is the "moral phenomenon" of Edenic purity shining through the young sailor's good looks that enrages him, and that rage, irreducible to any psychic drive or conflict, manifests what Melville, appealing to both Plato and the Bible, calls "a depravity according to nature," something "born with [Claggart] and innate," a "mystery of iniquity." Denis seems willing to make Galoup's murderous rage more psychologically intelligible. "I was jealous of Sentain," Galoup writes in his diary—jealous of everyone's, and especially Forestier's, esteem for Sentain. Forestier commends Sentain for saving one of his fellow Legionnaires from drowning after a burning helicopter crashes into the sea. The father's emphasis on the fraternal bond fortifies a fratricidal impulse: Forestier's public praise of Sentain as a model Legionnaire confirms and strengthens the hostility Galoup has felt since Sentain's arrival as part of a band of new recruits.

It is tempting to read Galoup's immediate antagonism as the symptom of a repressed homosexual desire, especially in light of Denis's definition, in the course of an interview, of desire as violence. *Beau travail* specifies this general formula. Faithful to the spirit of her commission, Denis identifies foreignness as the cause of violent desire. But who or what, exactly, is foreign? It is Sentain's supposed difference that awakens Galoup's murderous fascination. At the same time, however, his desire "picks up" Forestier as its object. Forestier, Galoup writes, has a mysterious past (including perhaps some scandal during his military career in Algeria). He is without ideals and, unlike Galoup, is indifferent to his special identity as a Legionnaire.

Intrinsically violent desire is desire in search of an object. It has to be objectified, but how it is objectified is almost a matter of indifference. Sentain's and Forestier's gendered identity, as well as their fantasmatic familial identities (younger brother and father) are secondary attributes of their impenetrability, of their differential otherness. But their very difference is perhaps invented in order to make another difference visible, a hatred and impenetrable difference within Galoup himself. As part of his voice-over, Galoup announces: "We all have a trash can deep within," which may be as close as Galoup comes to an accurate identification of the cause of his desire. That "trash can" travels, takes on recognizable sexual and social disguises, but no object could ever embody a constitutively unembodied otherness that is at once an alien self within the world and an alien world within the self.

The violence of *Beau travail* is the movement of the trash can to know and to master itself. But there is nothing to know, nothing to master, and in a sense, Galoup's hatred, like Claggart's, is irreducible to psychic content. But between Melville and Denis there is psychoanalysis, which breaks definitively with the vocabulary of depravity and iniquity. The account of the human given by psychoanalysis is closer to ontology than it is to psychology or morality. The mysterious revulsion aroused by the goodness of being can no longer be relegated to and sequestered within the ethical category of an evil innate to and occasionally visible within the human. Galoup is engaged in the rageful pursuit of being, of an otherness (which may be nothing but a void) that is constitutive of subjectivity itself. The narrative of appropriation nonetheless unfolds, although it has already been completed as failure. The unknown, inaccessible, imaginary self is enacted as a tragedy of failed, misplaced appropriation. While the type of movement exemplified by Galoup's persecution of Sentain is aimless—the desire that motivates it is intrinsically objectless—it is nonetheless articulated as a direction and a goal. It seeks to remove and destroy Sentain as the fantasized obstacle to Galoup's possession of Forestier's desire. There are moments, or stages, in this story: the perception of difference in Sentain and in Forestier, Galoup's exasperation at his inability to penetrate those differences, the plot to destroy, the consummation and failure of that plot, and the expulsion of Galoup from the family-world that has been his only home and his only identity.

What is most remarkable about Denis's film is that it juxtaposes the violence of desire with a kind of movement from which desire is absent. The film begins with images of native women dancing in a club frequented by Legionnaires, who move rhythmically around the women as momentary partners. The women and the Legionnaires don't dance in couples; each person is both dancing alone and participating in the rhythm of a mildly sensual sociability. (The only example of sexual coupling in the film is Galoup's apparent affair with one of the women.) Women, however, are mostly absent from the sensual sociality in *Beau travail*. It is, rather, the movements performed by the Legionnaires that most forcefully enact this sociality.

There is no story included in the images of the Legionnaires' life; apart from the suggestion of something special about Sentain to which the others are drawn, Denis makes no attempt to individualize them psychologically. At the beginning, she visually presents several of them to us, panning from one face to another, but this provides nothing deeper, or presumably more significant, than a physical identification. Though one black member of the group attends a Muslim prayer meeting in the village near their camp, the function of this incident is clearly not to tell us something about the Legionnaire himself, but to initiate the sequence of events that will lead to Galoup's betrayal of Sentain. The Legionnaires do, however, enact nonpsychological designifying movements as the film progresses. The first exercises we see them perform are obviously intended to prepare them for combat missions. The fast crawling under wires; the jumping over obstacles and in and out of ditches; and the exercise in which, carrying their rifles, they simulate taking possession of a building where enemies might be hidden—all this is part of their military training. We also see them as members of a self-sufficient domestic household: cutting each other's hair, hanging up clothes to dry, setting the table for meals, shaving, ironing. The positioning of the men in the last two of these activities points not only to a documentary intention (Legionnaires are expected, for example, to be as good at ironing their clothes as at their exercises in military preparedness), but also to the filmmaker's wish to compose images of the group that aestheticize their communal activities. The ways that the men are placed together (in contrast to the images of Galoup ironing and shaving alone) suggest in the early scenes that Denis will be less interested in telling us about the Legionnaires than in using them for a filmic experiment in bodily relatedness.

This becomes clearer in startlingly original ways in the second half of the film, once the group has moved and is setting up quarters on an arid plateau overlooking the sea and facing three volcanic formations rising from the water. Galoup admits to using the pretext of the Legionnaires being enlisted to repair a road in this desolate part of the country in order to separate Sentain from Forestier (who apparently stays behind). More important, Denis uses Galoup's calculation as a narrative justification for removing the Legionnaires from all social contacts, from any purpose whatsoever except to reinvent their own being-together.

The exercises we now see have no clearly discernible combat function; they prepare the Legionnaires for nothing except the sociality being improvised by their bodies in their choreographed movements. The choreography demilitarizes them; it at once betrays the official mission of documenting the Foreign Legion and is profoundly faithful to the intention of representing another sort of foreignness, a foreignness perhaps always hidden within them as a potentiality and that we now see them dance into the surfaces of their bodies. I'm thinking of the Legionnaires forming a circle around Galoup, then moving toward and away from him in short rapid steps. And there is the extraordinary scene in which each Legionnaire flings himself into the arms of another Legionnaire with whom he has been paired for the exercise; each pair repeats several times the rushing together and a rapid movement away from the other's body. Finally, when we see them in the more conventional activity of a rapidly paced march, the official training purpose of the march is undercut by the incongruous and ironic musical accompaniment of Neil Young's "Safeway Cart."

In describing the embracing exercise I write "paired" instead of "coupled" to avoid any suggestion of a sexual bonding between one Legionnaire and another as the grounding of their collective sociality. Indeed, it is as if the very possibility of such an intimacy is exhausted by the exhausting repetition of a strenuous and fundamentally indifferent coming together. An energetic choreography stifles the movements of desire before they can become psychic designs. Sensuality, depsychologized, is prevented from mutating into the sexual. The pleasures into which the Legionnaires exercise themselves are nonpurposive pleasures of touch, of each body having its place in a formal, mobile unity of communal repetition. The men, Rob White has written in a perceptive essay on *Beau travail*, are not masking violence; rather, they engage in "a shadow theater of violence in order to achieve mere gesture," thereby evacuating meaning. The Legionnaires' progressively more choreographed bodies initiate what Foucault calls a "new relational mode," an as yet contentless sociality that seductively sets the stage for the invention of other manifestations of nonsadistic movement, both within the individual psyche and between the human subject and the world.

In the Legionnaires' movements, something is stilled. It is the imminently violent restlessness of Galoup's psyche, the chaotic lurching of his desire (toward Sentain, toward Forestier, toward himself). Galoup's small, compact body is a package of withheld movement, the cage that imprisons his murderous passions until his desire, always on the watch, finds the moment when it can strike out. That moment is, of course, when he sees how he might destroy Sentain (and, more profoundly, himself).

Remarkably, the unleashing of his violent impulses is not only played out within the narrative of *Beau travail*; like what opposes it (the choreographic being-together of those he calls his flock), it is also danced. Lying on his bed after his expulsion from the Legion, holding the gun he may use on himself, in the film's final sequence Galoup metamorphoses from the pulse we see beating in his arm to the frantic energy of his wild accompaniment to the music of Corona's 1995 disco hit "Rhythm of the Night." The music begins softly while the camera is still focused on Galoup's arm; it continues, much louder, when the scene switches to Denis's choreographic metaphor (also Galoup's fantasy? or hallucination?) for violent desire no longer contained. He is back in the club where we saw the Legionnaires and the women dancing, but he is alone, his only partner appropriately his own reflection in the diamond-patterned mirror. He begins his response to the music slowly, then quickly accelerates into frenzied jumping and rolling across the floor and out of the left side of the frame, returns a few seconds later to roll spasmodically toward the right, and finishes, curiously, by suddenly standing just before he leaves the screen.

It is as if, at this final moment, the actor, Denis Lavant, were stepping out of his role just before the camera stops filming him. The abruptness of this normalizing of Galoup emphasizes the fantasmatic nature of his plot. Given the sociality performed by the Legionnaires, there is something gratuitous, perhaps even unnecessary, about the violent family drama he has set in motion. It is unlikely that the trash can within—within all of us—can ever be eliminated, but its obscene destructiveness can be modulated by way of a rejection of the familial imperatives that are its principal socializing vehicle. Director Denis ends her film with what seems to me a momentous possibility, a new imperative: stand up and simply leave the family tragedy by which Western culture has been oppressed at least since Oedipus's parricide. An unintended parricide, a fact that seems to have been forgotten once it became a complex presumably necessary (as Lacan relentlessly insists in his seminar on the psychoses) in order for the human to give birth to the social. Leave the violence of a desire for the father and the son, a violence that transforms brotherhood into fratricide.

Small wonder that Denis multiplies witnesses to the collective psychic rebirth her film implicitly calls for. There is not only her film audience. Within *Beau travail* we see, at certain moments, groups of Africans standing nearby or riding in a minibus, simply watching the Legionnaires as they work or exercise. In a grander dimension, there are the impressive still shots of the mountains and the sea surrounding the Legionnaires' camp, images of nature itself in a kind of stilled contemplation of humanity both destroying and renewing itself. Finally, there is the witnessing manifested by this discussion of *Beau travail*. Without claiming that it rivals the beautiful piece of work that is Denis's film (or the "beautiful find," as Forestier calls the orphan Sentain, abandoned and discovered in a stairwell), I would like my own exercise in witnessing to be taken as an admittedly exalted collaboration with the children who refuse the family game imposed on them, children who insist, in their play, on the foreignness of that game and on their determination to remain orphans.

2 · · · · · · · · · · · ·

ILLEGITIMACY

What does it mean to be a man? But first of all, what does it mean to act like a man? And, most important, what is the relation between acting like a man and being a man? We have become so used to thinking of masculinity and femininity as cultural constructions, and gender-bending has become, in the world of fashion as well as in queer theory and practice, such a familiar alternative to gender trouble that it has become difficult if not impossible for us to take seriously—by which I mean literally—the questions just asked. And yet they were taken seriously, and literally, by a writer who has become for some of us an icon of the thinking, and in particular the queer thinking, that has made such questions obsolete.

I'm thinking of Jean Genet, the *avant la lettre* gender bender par excellence. For Genet, the so-called real is, it would seem, inseparable both from the names we give to it and the gestures by which we stage it. And for Genet, masturbation is the master gender bender; alone in his bleak jail cell, he masturbates the fabulous beings of his great novel, *Our Lady of the Flowers* (1943), into existence. And let's not qualify that by saying "into a merely literary existence." Genet's fantasmatic performativity is at the same time Genet's ontology. Sartre showed his ambivalent respect for Genet's masturbatory power by calling him an essentialist. "Genet's imagination is essentialist," Sartre wrote, "as is his homosexuality. . . . He generates each of his characters out of a higher Essence; he reduces the episode to being merely the manifest illustration of an eternal truth." Genet names not merely to illustrate an essence but to change being.

Gestures function in the same way. "Resting against the cushions of a carriage," Sartre writes, Divine, the fabulous queen-whore of Pigalle, who is at the center of Genet's novel, "is in a position analogous to that of an infanta; therefore she *is* an infanta." To be like something is the animating force of a metamorphosis; "as for the medieval clerk," Sartre concludes, "apparent analogy is [for Genet] a sign of deep identity."[1]

My interest in Genet might seem incompatible with what I want to present as the question to which my discussion will offer some tentative answers: How can we become unnamable? The question is important if, as I believe, unnamability can operate as a form of resistance to networks of repressive power. With Genet, however, we are far from moving forward in a quest for unnamability, or so it would seem. Indeed, the very freedom with which Genet, in his exalted masturbatory fantasies, transforms and creates being through names and gestures subjects being to a kind of nominalist enslavement. The very negation of a nonperformative real impoverishes the real by framing it within the semantic confines of a name. There is no unaccountable contingency that might break into the frame, no supplemental reality that might insinuate itself into the margins of essentialized being, no event that might disrupt or exceed the named event. It therefore becomes all the more interesting to note those instances when the demiurgic drive fails.

There are comical moments when being fails to follow naming—moments analogous to those when the most carefully elaborated masturbatory fantasy doesn't do the job, is flaccidly rebuffed by the nonresponsive equipment it is meant to activate. Divine is smitten with the young male murderer called Our Lady of the Flowers. "Until then," Genet notes, Divine "had loved only men who were stronger and just a little, a tiny bit older, and more muscular than herself." But something different happens with

1. Jean-Paul Sartre, Introduction to Jean Genet, *Our Lady of the Flowers,* trans. Bernard Frechtman (New York, Grove, 1963), 32–35.

Our Lady. A "feeling of power" springs up in Divine; "she thought," Genet writes, "she had been virilified." Her amorous hope "made her strong and husky and vigorous. She felt muscles growing," and then, "bolder still," she wants to box, but she quickly gets knocked about on the boulevard by men whose movements, unlike Divine's, are willed not by an aesthetic of maleness but for their "combative efficiency." "She tried for male gestures, which," Genet unexpectedly asserts, "are rarely the gestures of males."

> She whistled, put her hands into her pockets, and this whole performance was carried out so unskillfully that in the course of a single evening she seemed to be four or five characters at the same time. She therefore acquired the richness of a multiple personality. She ran from boy to girl, and the transitions from one to the other—because the attitude was a new one— were made stumblingly. She would hop after the boy on one foot. She would always begin her Big Scatterbrain gestures, then, suddenly remembering that she was supposed to show she was virile so as to capture the murderer, she would end by burlesquing them, and this double formula enveloped her in strangeness, made her a timid clown in plain dress, a sort of embittered swish.[2]

So there is, apparently, a maleness beyond male gestures, perhaps something like a real male essence that can't be linguistically, gesturally, aesthetically called into existence, a male being out of the reach of a theatrics of maleness. Maleness may exist, surprisingly, before it is willfully essentialized. "Existence precedes essence" became a popular Sartrean slogan, and while Sartre's brilliant reading attributes to Genet an anti-Sartrean reversal of that formula, Genet may, at least at certain moments, be an existentialist in spite of himself.[3] Males only rarely have the gestures

---

2. Genet, *Our Lady*, 132–34; hereafter abbreviated *LF*.

3. See Jean-Paul Sartre, *Saint-Genet, comédien et martyr* (Paris: Éditions Gallimard, 1952). The introduction to Frechtman's English translation of Genet's novel is taken from this study.

of males; their existence as males may not require an essence of maleness, and no amount of essentializing naming will ever catch up with that existence.

But how, exactly, do males manifest themselves? Is so-called maleness nothing but an unnamable resistance to identitarian and essentializing naming? If, in the case of Genet, we decide not to drop the category of maleness altogether, it may be because he can't be reduced to the system of theatrical fantasmatics that seems to be a chief characteristic of his writing. The failures of language and gesture to coerce being into existence frictionalize fantasy with something we might be tempted to call reality, and the addition of friction to fiction would make it not entirely inappropriate to call Genet a realist.

What is the nature of that friction? In another passage of Genet's novel, we see Divine in a state of fury: she "would like to weep with rage, to tear cambric handkerchiefs with her nails and teeth" (*LF*, 220). She has spent the night in a cabaret with the two men who live with her, the black Gorgui, who is "her man" (*LF*, 217), and the young and pretty assassin Our Lady, with whom, as I have said, Divine has become infatuated. Gorgui, wearing tails and a white tie, treats Our Lady, in drag for the occasion, as his date. At 5 A.M., going home, they walk down the Rue Lepic like a couple, Our Lady holding Gorgui by the arm, while Divine, forgotten and murderously and doubly jealous, stays behind pretending to fasten a garter. Divine is humiliated even more when Gorgui steps aside in order to let Our Lady be the first to enter a taxi, then gets in himself, leaving Divine outside until, already settled, he invites her to join them. To save her dignity, Divine has to think quickly, but in order to do so she has to make a quick gender change. "For, though she felt as a 'woman,'" Genet writes, "she thought as a 'man.'" This does not mean that "in thus reverting spontaneously to her true nature, Divine was a male wearing make-up, disheveled with make-believe gestures." Indeed, her "femininity was not *only* a masquerade," although, for Genet, it is hardly invalidated in being a masquerade. If "all the 'woman' judgments she made were, in reality, poetical conclusions," it is only at such moments that Divine was "true." But—this convoluted explanation proceeds—"to think is to perform an act. In order to act you have to discard frivolity and set your idea on a solid base. So she was aided by the idea of solidity, which she associated with the idea of virility." Not only that: when she is with Mimosa, her Pigalle sister-queen, both of whom use the feminine in addressing each other, Divine "managed to think 'woman' with regard to serious but never essential things" (*LF*, 224–225).

Seen in conjunction with the boxing-whistling passage, all this makes for quite a gender jumble. In desiring Our Lady as a feminized sexual partner, Divine feels "virilified," but she can't, through her actions, attain the male identity that would apparently be the necessary support for her desires. Divine is too much the queen to reach the maleness necessary to become Our Lady's "imperious" lover; on the other hand, Divine, originally Louis Culafroy, is physically a man—a fact eluded in the first passage but central to the second. A man masquerading as a woman incapable of becoming the male she must be in order to act on her virile desires. Man needs maleness in order to behave like a man, but the deftly performed masquerade as woman defeats what is apparently another masquerade needed to make the body conform to its own nature. And there is in Genet a bodily nature outside performance, or, if not exactly a nature, something intractably resistant to the real but ultimately limited power of poetry.

I haven't yet cited the most startling sentence of the second passage. While insisting that Divine's femininity wasn't only a masquerade (an "only" that is, from Genet, somewhat strange), Genet goes on to explain: "But as for thinking 'woman' completely, her organs hindered her" (*LF*, 225). If they weren't enough to allow Divine to attain maleness, they are sufficient to prevent her from being entirely a woman. Genet's worship of the cock brings into his work a strong sense of the body, of both its complicity with and resistance to the comedy of identity. The body provides the masturbatory point of departure for an extravagant identitarian mobility, but it also sets limits to the very masquerade to which, once stimulated, it gives rise.

In a universe that celebrates the power of fantasy elaborated and, in a sense, materialized in language, a universe in which naming creates being, the body provides—infrequently, it's true—a gravitational force that contravenes the centrifugal multiplication of words and gestures. It is as if it had its own intentionality, one that erodes the essentializing freedom of the imaginary. As a result, the categories of man and woman, and of maleness and femaleness, while they remain the central structuralizing principles of Genet's fantasmatic productivity, also enter into an unresolved, unsynthesized frictional dialectics of identity, one in which, astonishingly enough, the regal naming of being can go adrift in something like the burlesque strangeness of Divine running, or more accurately stumbling, as Genet puts it, from boy to girl, and back again. Neither one nor the other, Divine is reduced to "a timid clown in plain dress, a sort of embittered swish," but that pathetically muddled figure has, in its very muddlement, become unnamable, free by virtue of its very failure to be recognized, to be identified.

"The State . . . brings into existence by naming and distinguishing."[4] These words, which appear on the final page of Pierre Bourdieu's 1997 *Pascalian Meditations,* condense the lessons of Bourdieu's lifelong work of exposing the hierarchical system of classification by which the social order identifies and legitimizes our social existence. We are distinguished—made distinct from one another—by the attitudes, beliefs, and behaviors assigned to the social stratum or class to which each of us belongs. The boundaries separating social modes of being define and limit the field of permissible mobility within the elaborately designed map of

---

4. Pierre Bourdieu, *Pascalian Meditations,* trans. Richard Nice (Stanford, Calif.: Stanford University Press, 2000), 245.

social classification by social class. What makes this system of classificatory control work is, according to Bourdieu, its internalization by those subjected to it. We recognize the identity imposed on us as always already ours. "Objective limits," Bourdieu writes in *Distinction* (1979), "become a sense of limits, . . . a 'sense of one's place' which leads one to exclude oneself from the goods, persons, places and so forth from which one is excluded."[5] Bourdieu criticizes the Sartrean view of "the social gaze [*le regard social*]" as "a universal, abstract, objectifying power." Rather, he says, we should understand that gaze as "a social power, whose efficacy is always partly due to the fact that the receiver recognizes the categories of perception and appreciation it applies to him or her."[6] The extraordinary inertia resulting from the inscription of social structures on our bodies accounts for the difficulty of escaping from those structures.

The process of identificatory classification is of course also one of legitimization. A name behaves in a certain way; to the extent that we recognize the name socially transmitted to us as ours, as carrying our authentic identity, we endorse the judgments inherent in the classifying system, judgments that can be proscriptive as well as prescriptive. A hierarchy of distinctions includes nonlegitimized groups. The operative distinctions tend, Bourdieu writes, to separate what should be separated and to bring together what, it is judged, should be brought together, and this means that unions outside the definition of what constitutes a legitimate union are classified as unions "against nature." The antinature argument—which could be thought of as the legitimating alibi for a profound classificatory bias—is of course familiar to us in heterosexist polemics against gay and lesbian marriage and especially gay and lesbian adoptions. Such unions, Bourdieu writes, give rise to "visceral, murderous horror, absolute disgust, metaphysical fury" for "everything which passes understanding

5. Pierre Bourdieu, *Distinction: A Social Critique of the Judgement of Taste,* trans. Richard Nice (Cambridge, Mass.: Harvard University Press, 1984), 471.

6. Ibid., 207.

[*tout ce qui passe l'entendement*]"[7]—an interesting way of formulating a disgust that, while presenting itself as grounded in immutable laws of nature, is in reality a rageful rejection of any social arrangement threatening the bodily incorporated principles that constitute how we understand the world, that give to the social world an indispensable intelligibility. From this perspective, gay marriage is a serious, unacceptable transgression of relational classifications outside of which, it is implicitly claimed, we could no longer make sense of the social world.

What are the possibilities of escaping from this classificatory prison of sense? The transgression of boundaries is, it seems to me, merely a rearrangement (and not even a provisional erasure) of the social map. It is not, for example, that gay marriage is an inadequate transgression of the social order; rather, the problem is that it is *only* a transgression. It does nothing to question the given institutional legitimization of intimacy; it would make the institution more inclusive without attacking its right to authenticate, to officially testify to its participants' privileged rank in the relational hierarchy. It has been argued that gay marriage could subvert the institution from within, change the terms by which it is, at least officially, recognized and differentiated from other types of relation. But why keep the category if its identifying terms become unrecognizable? What is the limit at which marriage would lose so many of its recognized attributes that it would no longer make any sense to get married? Are we at least clear, among ourselves, that our only valid defense of gay marriage is a practical—more specifically, a legal—one?

The generally unexpressed truth is of course that marriage, as a heterosexually constituted classification, will have no trouble at all competing against whatever new or, as we like to say, subversive attributes a proud gay and lesbian imagination may bring to it. The historical weight of what has been historically legitimated

7. Ibid., 475. Bourdieu, *Distinction: Critique sociale du jugement* (Paris: Les Éditions de Minuit, 1979), 553.

as marriage will have no trouble crushing or assimilating our queer inventiveness, however perverse we may will our inventions to be. Contrary to the conviction of many American lawmakers, we don't need a legislative defense of heterosexual marriage. History has already made it a nearly impregnable fortress impossible to take (even when its particular contractual terms are violated). However, it is a fortress that might simply be deserted.

Bourdieu has his own exit from imprisoning names. Toward the end of *Pascalian Meditations*, he writes that objectively imposed and subjectively recognized and incorporated limits can be transgressed to the extent that subversive speech and action, "attentive to the real chances of transforming the power relation, . . . are able to work to raise expectations beyond the objective chances on which they spontaneously tend to be aligned, but without pushing them beyond the threshold where they would become unreal and foolhardy." If, as Bourdieu claims, symbolic transgression of a social frontier has in itself a liberating effect of articulating what has until then been the unthinkable, that effect depends on the contested structures already being "in a state of uncertainty and of crisis" that would create conditions favorable to "an awakening of critical consciousness of their arbitrariness and fragility."[8] Effective transgression thus becomes a delicate balancing act between useful and useless aspirations, as well as between moments of structural stability and other moments— to be seized and exploited—of structural uncertainty. A productively frictional relation between different fields of analytic research would presumably increase the probability of accurate judgments of when subversive ambitions would or would not be symbolically practical, as well as of the historically determined waxing and waning of power structures.

The principal adjudicator in all this would be the sociologist, certainly not the classically trained sociologist who is still, at least in the French university, the agent of greatest power, but rather

8. Bourdieu, *Pascalian Meditations,* 236.

the sociologist best exemplified by, I would suppose, Bourdieu himself. While Bourdieu's work on the repressively creative function of social naming and the correlative power of defining and legitimating social identities is invaluable, the discipline within which he did this work could, it seems to me, provide only inadequate formulas of resistance. Bourdieu's emphasis on the subject's complicity with the identity imposed on him or her— we recognize as already ours the names imposed on us—is an important aspect of his work. But any analysis of the psychic processing of social naming must include factors alien to a strictly sociological perspective on the mind, which only psychoanalysis can provide.

To recognize as belonging to us that which limits and oppresses us is a phenomenon impoverished by the word used to describe it. Recognition is the conscious end-term of hidden impulses that complicate it, that make our apparently complicitous recognitions an ambiguous mix of an erotically charged desire to be controlled as well as a nostalgic fantasy of lost authentic being that might energize a resistance to available social terms of understanding. These psychic phenomena at once fortify our subjection to an oppressive intelligibility and contain versions of potential being that constitutively resist that given intelligibility. The very recognition of the recognition described by Bourdieu is already an aspect of that resistance, although it is probably also identical, in the logic of the (psychoanalytically rather than sociologically described) unconscious, to that from which it seeks to liberate us. An awareness of these conflicting impulses to resist subjection and to resist that resistance—essentially, a taking into account of the unconscious—is indispensable to the political relevance of social analysis.

How to resist the naming that confers legitimacy? Bourdieu's study of how naming can either legitimize or delegitimize social identities has led me to think about the possibly great value of a delegitimized social existence. I don't mean subverting or transgressing the boundaries of legitimacy; rather, we might accept delegitimization as a nullifying of the naming authority itself. The Law that names us, that legitimizes or delegitimizes the identities it names, is not an agency that can be negotiated with, and to reject its authority may necessitate a potentially irreversible negativizing not only of the world but also of the subject him- or herself. This unqualified negativity (I should add that my negativizing impulse, somewhat dormant, or equivocated, since the Genet chapter of my book *Homos*, has been reinvigorated—if that can be said about such impulses—by Lee Edelman's compelling case for "no future") has, astonishingly, been represented in a film I will be discussing in a moment, but first let's briefly pay tribute to the more workable if also more limited strategy of a subversively excessive assumption, or taking on, of the names imposed on us.[9]

Foucault, arguing that a psychiatric discourse of the second half of the nineteenth century created the homosexual as a characterological entity—a psychic structure that, having been made visible, could be dissected, manipulated, disciplined—also spoke of a "reverse discourse." By that he meant that homosexuality, almost contemporaneously with its invention, "began to speak in its own behalf, to demand that its legitimacy or 'naturality' be acknowledged, often in the same vocabulary, using the same categories by which it was disqualified," thus challenging the power structures responsible for its creation.[10] Gay pride and perhaps also gay marriage are expressions of this demand, and while recognizing all there is to applaud in the former, the latter may be the logical end point, as I suggested a moment ago in different terms, of our remaining, however transgressively, within the discourse that has disqualified us. Our indebtedness to that discourse in our very subversion of it leaves us vulnerable to its appeal, to

9. See Leo Bersani, *Homos* (Cambridge, Mass.: Harvard University Press, 1995), and Lee Edelman, *No Future: Queer Theory and the Death Drive* (Durham, N.C.: Duke University Press, 2004).

10. Michel Foucault, *The History of Sexuality*, vol. 1: *An Introduction*, trans. Robert Hurley (New York: Pantheon, 1978), 101.

the versions of legitimacy seductively implicit in the vocabulary and categories that define our willed *il*legitimacy. That Foucault may have realized something of the sort seems indicated by his injunction, a century after the reverse discourse began to make itself be heard, that we invent "new relational modes" and, most tellingly, by his reminder that "we have to work at becoming homosexuals."[11]

Finally, more spectacularly but also less consequentially, there is Genet's transgressive adherence to the terms that excluded and condemned him. According to Sartre's well known argument, Genet chooses the evil attributed to him, which means that he has "to affirm the pre-existence of good"—even more, to make himself both the judged one and the judge. "Incapable," Sartre writes, "of *carving out* a place in the universe for himself, he *imagines* in order to convince himself that he has created the world which excludes him."[12] The escape from a judging world in the form of a total, willed immersion in it is at the extreme limit of subversive parody. Genet's demiurgic power would be to reinvent a world already given to him; his self-fashioning, however rebellious its intention, is no less a tautology. In contrast to this, Divine's comic and pathetic stumbling between maleness and femaleness in *Our Lady of the Flowers* at least momentarily nullifies the very categories in which—and this may be her tragic flaw—she seeks to be immobilized.

What is the subject of Todd Haynes's 1995 film, *Safe*? Who is the subject of *Safe*? Carol White, who lives with her husband, Greg, and her stepson in a well-to-do community in the San Fernando Valley, develops an increasingly acute allergy to her surroundings. One morning, in a moment of apparent weakness and fa-

---

11. Michel Foucault, "Friendship as a Way of Life," in Michel Foucault, *Ethics: Subjectivity and Truth,* trans. Robert Hurley and others, ed. Paul Rabinow (New York: New Press, 1997), 136.

12. Jean-Paul Sartre, *Saint Genet: Actor and Martyr* (Minneapolis: University of Minnesota Press, 2012), 468.

tigue, she stumbles in her living room after walking through her kitchen where a couple of tradespeople are working and her maid is spraying polish on dishware. Shortly after that, as she is driving on a freeway, fumes from a truck give her a fit of violent coughing. Her symptoms worsen and become frequent: a serious nosebleed at the hairdresser's, attacks of asthma at a party and in the course of a series of allergy tests, and, at the dry cleaner's, a seizure that leads to a stay in the hospital. Her doctor can't find anything wrong with her, and a session with a psychiatrist is flatly unproductive.

After seeing a flier at her health club that begins with the questions "Do you smell fumes? Are you allergic to the twentieth century?," Carol goes to a meeting where a man on a TV monitor speaks about the environmental illness caused when our natural tolerance to everyday chemicals breaks down. This seems to put Carol on the right track: her first attack followed her exposure to the fumes from the truck just ahead of her car, and her nosebleed occurred after her hair had been soaked in the chemicals used during a permanent. She meets other people also suffering from the effects of toxins in the environment, and at another meeting a woman speaks of the need to create an oasis, a safe, toxin-free place. Finally, at the hospital she hears on TV about Wrenwood, a retreat in New Mexico that its founder, Peter Dunning, describes as "a safe haven for troubled times." Carol decides to join the Wrenwood community, where a group of people, all having been afflicted with chemical or affective toxins that made it impossible for them to continue living in the "normal" world, lead a peaceful, healthy, communally supportive and apparently contented existence, and where therapy consists of both their physical isolation and group sessions in the New Age philosophy propounded by Peter.

Peter's lesson is simple and radical: we are the cause of our illnesses; we see outside what we feel within; self-transformation will bring global transformation. The success of this therapy is far from evident, with a couple of exceptions (most notably Claire, the at-peace-with-herself-and-with-the-world director of the center), although we see only one case of rebellious resistance to Peter's teaching. As for Carol, she goes along sympathetically, if passively, with the Wrenwood philosophy until the end of the film even though there is very little sign of physical improvement. On the contrary: she has to carry an oxygen tank at all times, her face is gaunt and her skin splotched, and finally she has to leave her cabin, still too exposed to poisons from the outside, and take what may be permanent refuge in a small, white, windowless, porcelain-lined, almost furniture-free, igloo-like structure that leaves her sequestered even from the sequestered Wrenwood community, alone with the self that is, she has been taught to believe, both the source of her illness and a possible cure.

It has been argued both that *Safe* is and that it is not a metaphor or an allegory for AIDS. Haynes's film takes place in 1987, during the worst period of the epidemic. AIDS, very much in the public awareness at the time, is mentioned a few times in the film, especially in one instance when Haynes appears to be encouraging us to see some connection between Carol's affliction and HIV infection. In an early scene, Carol's best friend, Linda, talks to her about her unmarried brother's recent death; in what we might take as an unsurprising willful denial, she assures Carol that AIDS was not the cause. In the TV clip about Wrenwood, Peter mentions AIDS as one of "the diseases of our time," and shortly after Carol arrives at the retreat we learn that Peter himself has AIDS. What I find intriguing about the implied metaphoricity of Carol's illness is the nonchalantly accepted misfit between the two terms of the presumed metaphor. Rather than voting yes or no in the debate about AIDS as the implicit subject of the film, we might find the bad fit itself the most interesting aspect of the connection. During the first few minutes of the film we have an extended shot, filmed from above the bed, of Greg's back and Carol's face as they have missionary-position sex, or, more accurately, as Greg thrustingly makes his way toward sexual climax with a patient but clearly unexcited Carol. The scene obviously suggests something about their relationship. More interestingly, in purely sequential terms we can't help but note that Carol's symptoms begin to appear shortly thereafter. This certainly does not suggest that Greg has transmitted to Carol a disease of the immune system. Nevertheless, given what we know about the transmission of the HIV virus, and given the fact that both AIDS and Carol's "environmental illness" involve damage to and even breakdown of the immune defenses, that sequence—sex followed by an immune disorder—can't help but be at least teasingly fraught.

But why? In what way does Haynes's film profit from this inevitable yet largely gratuitous connection? The question of incongruous connectedness becomes more pronounced when we consider the relation between the Wrenwood and pre-Wrenwood sections of the film. The first part of *Safe* may, with some plausibility, be taken as a serious ecological argument. We are given statistical information about the degree to which the air we breathe has become chemically polluted, a pollution made no less shocking by the apparent (and perhaps deceptive) tolerance most of us have developed to it. Carol is frequently filmed in long shots; the camera slowly and ominously moves closer to her at the beginnings of her allergic attacks. Otherwise, seen from a distance she is visually little more than a human speck among the objects (such as the furniture in her living room) that occupy much more of the filmic frame than she does. Correlatively, her small, nonassertive voice is no match for the sounds (from radio and TV and the massive freeway traffic) that also assault her senses.

As has frequently been noted, Carol is a remote presence; the distance at which she is kept is psychological as well as visual. Haynes seems to have deliberately made her psychologically empty, without the inner life that classical cinema, especially with its close-ups of the human face, has made us take for granted as a necessary and defining characteristic of the human. But this very emptiness, the psychic absence as well as the physical insignificance, also makes plausible Carol's exceptional vulnerability to the toxins engulfing her. It is as if we were viewing an alien presence with no defenses against the world. Carol's thinness as a cinematic character allows her to serve very well as an allegorical model of an always imminent human breakdown in the poisonous spaces created by our industrious industrial activity.

Wrenwood appears to move us into another film. True, there are members of the community who have suffered an environmental illness like Carol's (Claire had lived "six miles from a chemical factory in Michigan that was leaking something like fifteen gallons of chemical by-product a day"), but others, as we learn in one of their therapy sessions, have been psychically poisoned: one by her guilt over her child's sickness, another, it is suggested, by being abused as a young girl. We have shifted to diverse forms of imbalance between the subject and the world, cases in which the subject has been nearly crushed by the strength of destructive energies—both human and nonhuman—in the world. The first part of the film could (but doesn't) steer in the direction of environmental activism. Wrenwood, more an escape than an activist response, is, in one sense, still within this field of meaning: it is meant to be an oasis, a toxin-free safe place urged as a flight from the environmental illnesses of those in the audience at one of the meetings Carol attends. Wrenwood is literally a retreat, and the logic of this response is spelled out in Peter's New Age teaching. All is well in the world if we love ourselves; what we see outside is nothing but a reflection of what we feel within. In one scene Peter tells his Wrenwood flock that he has stopped reading newspapers and watching the news on TV. "Media gloom and doom" are antithetical to his conviction, as he tells the one recalcitrant member of the community, that "the only person who can make you sick is you. . . . Whatever the sickness, if our immune system has been damaged, it's because we have allowed it to be."

Haynes is certainly not endorsing the most absurd conclusion to which Peter's teaching might be said to point: that environmental pollutions can be erased by self-love, a conclusion consistent with Peter's vision of a "global transformation" reflecting and coinciding with what he calls "the transformation I revel at within." It is perhaps because Haynes counts on his audience immediately retreating from this New Age gibberish that he can afford to present a sympathetic portrait of Wrenwood and its founder. There is no suggestion of hypocrisy or of a plot to financially exploit his followers (Peter's luxurious home, perhaps the sign of his profit-making enterprise, is visible to the admiring residents on a hill overlooking the community), and there appears to be no doubt about the sincerity of the director's attempts to help the residents cure themselves. Sincerity is, of course, no guarantee of effectiveness, and Haynes gives us very little reason to believe that the therapy is working. In a written direction placed just before Peter's outdoor meeting with the residents, Haynes indicates that "although everyone is saying the 'right' things there is a sadness that hangs in the air."[13] Peter asks a few members of the group to say what made them sick, and he unhesitatingly provides the cues for what are clearly the right answers.

Haynes's tact in his presentation of Wrenwood makes its relation to the first part of *Safe* even more problematic. Had he exposed his New Agers as hypocritical villains, the film might have had an uninteresting coherence: it would have been a case of people in great distress being intentionally deluded, at their material and emotional expense, into believing that they can simply will or love themselves out of their distress. In short, a sad story. More interesting is an incongruity similar, but on a larger structural scale, to the one between AIDS and environmental illness. The environmental perils of our present chemically saturated lives are of course not addressed by a New Age recourse to the power of self-love, but this hardly original message can't account for the power of Haynes's work. That power lies, it seem to me, hidden within the incongruous juxtaposition of the film's three major subjects: environmental illness, AIDS, and self-love. A familiar logic might dismiss the film, or at least diminish its status, for the very incongruity of its implicit sets of relations. HIV is a

13. Todd Haynes, *Far from Heaven, Safe, and Superstar: Three Screenplays* (New York: Grove, 2003), 173.

historically contingent syndrome (it could appear anywhere at any time), while environmental illness, to which sex is irrelevant, is a modern ailment resulting from industrial pollution. And while the inherent irrelevance of self-love to saving ourselves from HIV infection as well as environmental illness is clear, there *is* a way in which Peter's gospel of self-love applies to the different illnesses the film represents or evokes. It applies not as a cure, but as something more complicated and more sinister.

When Claire, Wrenwood's director, is consoling Carol, who has been crying alone in her cabin on the evening of her arrival, she tells her that she was unable even to walk when she first moved to the retreat and that she helped to cure herself by looking in the mirror every day and saying, "Claire, I *love* you, I really love you." In the film's extraordinary final scene, Haynes gives us a close-up of Carol looking at herself in the small mirror on the wall of her igloo home murmuring "I love you" several times in a barely audible, expressionless voice, and with a blank if perhaps futilely expectant face. The bleakness of the gray, bare interior of her perhaps final safe haven is emphasized by its contrast with the enjoyable evening of a dinner that she and a friendly male resident had just made for the group, followed by dancing and a surprise birthday cake to celebrate Carol's birthday. In the little speech she is coaxed into making after blowing out the candles on the cake, Carol inarticulately and approvingly summarizes the self-love lesson of Wrenwood—a lesson that is cruelly mocked a few moments later in the igloo mirror scene, in which Carol's proclamation of love to herself does nothing to alter the blank, gaunt, devastated features of a reflection that is unmoved, untouched by this climactic enactment of the Wrenwood cure.

In its apparent retreat from the world, Wrenwood is a parodistically faithful repetition of a major philosophical and psychoanalytic message about the world as dangerously alien to its human subjects. As I will argue more fully in the following chapter (centered on Descartes, Proust, and Freud), a turning away from the world in order to reject or control it through an autonomous subjectivity has been a major theme in modern Western thought. The ontological gap separating *res cogitans* from *res extensa* (Descartes), the world as a dismissible distraction in the aesthetic re-creation of it (Proust), and the perception of what is outside the subject as a threat to the willed coherence and unity of the subject's inherently fragile individualizing ego (Freud): some of the most compelling thinkers of our culture have encouraged us to think of our condition as one of Heideggerian thrownness into a world of enigmatically and dangerously differential otherness.

The power of *Safe* lies in its original restatement of this message. Environmental illness is not a metaphor for AIDS; both are contemporary reinforcements and vindications of the individualistic ideology of Wrenwood. The inspirational Peter is described to Carol as "a chemically sensitive person with AIDS." His sexually contracted illness is, like his chemical sensitivity, the result of intimate contacts with the world. As we have seen during the AIDS epidemic, the existence of a sexually transmitted, potentially fatal disease lends itself particularly well to political exploitation of a philosophical, aesthetic, and psychoanalytic argument concerning the essential foreignness of the world to its perhaps intrinsically estranged inhabitants. Especially during the early years of AIDS, we were repeatedly told that the best and safest protection against dangerous relations with others is to re-nounce intimate relations with them and to practice abstinence. And if abstinence must allow for some sexual practice, that practice will of course be masturbation—that is, sexual self-love. Thus gays were once again marginalized, this time with apparent scientific authorization, in order both to save us from a world that had become dangerous for us, and to save the world from the danger we embodied, a perennial danger that had now become biologically detectable in our bodies.

Wrenwood is the perfect servant of a political strategy designed by networks of power to isolate individuals from political life (unlocatable, impersonal in the Foucauldian sense of how power is exercised). In the episteme of a culture where Wrenwood thrives, self-knowledge occupies a privileged position in the field of knowability. Peter rejects the gloom and doom in which newspapers and TV traffic, and relies instead on the ideology of individualism (itself grounded in the notion of a fundamental opposition, or difference of being, between the subject and the world) to make a marginalizing or exclusionary strategy of power appear to be an opportunity for a rebellious triumph of individual freedom. Freedom, even autonomy, and at the limit the illusion of self-creation, is the realization of the *causa sui* project.

Safe is indeed "about" AIDS in the sense that it enacts as a voluntary retreat from society the banishment from the relational field of intimacy that a homophobic culture was able to present as a hygienic imperative, and that poor, mystified Peter sees as an opportunity for self-knowledge and self-love. Peter has learned how to love Peter, which also means that Peter has learned to make of his own peter the principal object of his desire. His cure for dangerous relations—a cure for himself and for others—is the oxymoron of a masturbatory relationality. In the terms I have used in discussing Genet and Bourdieu, AIDS reinforced the delegitimizing of gays (HIV became a new delegitimizing attribute). At the same time, in obeying the now medically authorized homophobic goal of removing us from sexuality (and especially nonmonogamous sexuality), the social order granted us a new kind of legitimacy: one earned by our acceptance of a masturbatory retreat, our acceptance of "Wrenwood" as providing the boundaries of our identity.

Finally, however, we shouldn't forget that it is Carol, not Peter, who is at the center of *Safe*. Carol the nonteacher, the nonspeaker. In her startling, inarticulate passivity, Carol retreats beyond Wrenwood, which is, after all, a community, one in which a peaceful sociality is practiced. She is the logic of the film's incongruous juxtaposition of a feminist social critique, a narrative of the deadly consequences of industrial capitalism, a parabolic representation of AIDS, and a philosophy of self-protective, self-sequestering self-love. Carol makes no conscious political choices; she is, constitutively, a refusal to belong, to be named. Haynes even suggests early in the film that apart from the social and environmental oppressiveness that victimizes her, she is in the wrong universe. I'm thinking of the two nearly identical sequences in which we see Carol walking and standing alone in her garden at night, scenes accompanied by prolonged, mournful musical chords that, here and elsewhere in the film, add something portentous beyond the film's diegetic literalness. This radical aloneness is emphasized by her moments of verbal stumbling, as if the language that makes her a social being were a violation of an intrinsic being-apart and silence. Carol enacts a shedding of identities that is also a shedding of the film's subjects: the strongly legitimized identity of a middle-class female home-maker, her identity as a victim of industrial waste, her symbolic identity as an immune-damaged carrier of a fatal infection, and finally, her particular (and particularly thin) psychic identity as a person. Paradoxically, it is Carol's stammering words of self-love at the end of the film that signal the shedding of a person who might be loved. There is no one there. Carol might adopt the title of Haynes's 2007 film about Bob Dylan as the rebuttal of "I love you": "I'm not there." Applied to Dylan, these words refer to identities so richly dispersed that they can't be embodied in a single actor; Dylan's life and career are embodied by five male actors as well as, magnificently, Cate Blanchett. In Carol's case, there is no one to embody. Claire had managed to attach a name to her declaration of self-love: "I love you, Claire." Carol stops at a faintly murmured and by now highly problematic "you."

Social legitimization by way of naming—conferring an identity —turns out to be the most dangerous toxin. The most serious environmental illness is environmental identity. In a sense, Carol is Haynes's fictive scapegoat, created to serve as a model of a nonviable yet somehow also necessary self-negativizing. Much less active than Sartre's Genet (who freely chooses the deviant identity imposed on him), Carol doesn't subversively parody the identity assigned to her; rather, she simply disappears from it.

As a lesson to all of us tempted by the joys of an often hard-won legitimacy (newly given to gays by marriage and children), one that when learned, however, we may no longer be tempted to subvert or to change, Carol, at the moment she weakly calls an absent "me-you" into being, transforms a social cipher and, implicitly, a social outcast into a barely existent body. It is up to us to decide—Haynes has brilliantly done more than enough—if that body harbors some as yet unnamed passion.

3 ·

"ARDENT MASTURBATION" (DESCARTES, FREUD, PROUST, ET AL.)

What is the status of ontological certainty in Descartes? A long tradition in Cartesian scholarship has taken that certainty for granted—even while frequently attacking the grounds of Descartes's apparently secure assurance of being. In the third of the seven sets of objections solicited by Descartes himself and published in the same volume as the first and second editions of the *Meditations* in 1641 and 1642, Hobbes (who had fled to France for political reasons in 1640) writes: "All philosophers make a distinction between a subject and its acts, i.e. between a subject and its properties and its essence." But Descartes, he objects, "is identifying the thing which understands with the intellect, which is a power of that which understands." I think, Descartes argues, therefore I am a thinking thing (a *res cogitans*); "I might as well say," Hobbes comments, "I am walking, therefore I am a walk."[1] Closer to us, Heidegger, in the critique of traditional ontological presuppositions that opens *Being and Time,* accuses Descartes of leaving "undetermined . . . the kind of Being which belongs to the *res cogitans*, or—more precisely—the meaning of the Being of the 'sum.'" Descartes came to suppose, according to Heidegger, that the certainty inherent in the

This chapter was previously published as "'Ardent Masturbation' (Descartes, Freud, and Others)" in *Critical Inquiry* 38, no. 1 (Autumn 2011).

1. René Descartes, *Meditations on First Philosophy with Selections from the Objections and Replies,* trans. and ed. John Cottingham (Cambridge: Cambridge University Press, 1996), 69–70.

cogito "exempted him from raising the question of the meaning of the Being which this entity possesses."[2]

An indubitable ontological certainty is the precondition, and justification, for Descartes's epistemological assurance. This connection between being and knowledge is crucial: however shaky or rudimentary Cartesian ontology may be, its nature is, in a sense, secondary to the assurance it gives Descartes in his fundamental project, as he puts it in the *Discourse on Method*, of distinguishing the true from the false. The certainty derived from the cogito is what allows Descartes "to reject shifting earth and sand in order to find rock or clay"—that is, to exercise fully and confidently his extraordinarily energetic, we might even say militant, will to know.[3] Indeed, Foucault goes so far as to identify the beginning of the modern age in the history of Western configurations of subjectivity with what he calls "the Cartesian moment," the moment of the prioritizing of knowledge to the detriment of what Foucault designates as "care of the self," or spirituality.[4]

Descartes's purpose, as Husserl emphasized, was "to ground science absolutely," and, we might add, to realize the acquisition, through science, of power over the world.[5] The steps to be followed for reaching truth, the criteria to be used for the testing of all propositions and the certainty of being—both the thinker's being and God's being—are the preliminary stages of an investigation into the laws of nature. ("These Meditations," Descartes wrote in a letter to his friend Marin Mersenne, "contain the entire foundation for my physics.")[6] They are the necessary ground of

2. Martin Heidegger, *Being and Time,* trans. John Macquarrie and Edward Robinson (Oxford: Blackwell, 1962), 46.

3. René Descartes, *Discourse on Method, Optics, Geometry, and Meteorology,* trans. Paul J. Olscamp (Cambridge, MA: 2001), 24.

4. Michel Foucault, *The Hermeneutics of the Subject: Lectures at the Collège de France, 1981–1982,* ed. Frédéric Gros, trans. Graham Burchell (New York: Picador, 2005), 17.

5. Edmond Husserl, *Cartesian Meditations: An Introduction to Phenomenology,* trans. Dorion Cairns (The Hague: Martinus Nijhoff, 1970), 8.

6. Quoted in Daniel Garber, "*Semel in vita*: The Scientific Background to Des-

the exciting enterprise that will allow us to become, as Descartes formulates it in the final section of the *Discourse*, "masters and possessors . . . of nature."[7] Such is Descartes's ambition, and, it has generally been recognized, such is his modernity: a boundless confidence in the possibilities of rational scientific inquiry. The weakness of Descartes's mechanistic account of the laws of physics and the subsequent changes in both the methodology of the sciences and the confidence regarding our ability to master and possess nature do nothing to reduce Descartes's seminal importance in the historical prioritizing of scientific knowledge.

There is, however, something else, something missed even if we have adequately formulated both the weaknesses and the originality of Descartes's thought, and his importance in the history of modern philosophy. We should, I think, find something at once strange and familiar in our experience of reading Descartes. In discussing the *Meditations*, Bernard Williams, among others, makes a distinction between the author René Descartes and "the thinker,"—"the 'I' that appears throughout [the *Meditations*] from the first sentence on [and who] does not specifically represent" the author. The author "is not answerable for every notion entertained by the thinker and for every turn that the reflection takes on the way."[8] For Williams, the distinction between the author and the thinker (or, as L. Aryeh Kosman has put it, between the author and the naive narrator)[9] is that the latter, unlike the former, doesn't know, as he goes along, how the argument will turn out, and this fiction expresses Descartes's "intention to engage the reader in the argument." He "aims to convince us by making the argument ourselves" (thus presumably giving us the freedom to write the *Meditations* differently), and in so doing to show our-

cartes' *Meditations*," in *Essays on Descartes' Meditations*, ed. Amélie Oksenberg Rorty (Berkeley: University of California Press, 1986), 82.

7. Descartes, *Discourse*, 50.

8. Bernard Williams, "Introductory Essay," in Descartes, *Meditations*, vii.

9. See L. Aryeh Kosman, "The Naïve Narrator: Meditation in Descartes' *Meditations*," in *Essays*, ed. Rorty, 21–43.

selves to be "the kind of creatures [the thinking things] that [the book] finally shows us to be."[10]

Williams's distinction is useful, but it seems to me that the foregrounding of the thinker may have less to do with engaging the reader in the movement of the argument than with a certain movement on the part of the thinker himself in his search for the steps of the argument. Let's look at the beginning of the third meditation. I'm less interested here in what the Cartesian thinker has discovered (I am a thing that thinks; whatever I perceive very clearly and distinctly is true; sensory perception can deceive us regarding the correspondence between our ideas and the things outside me) than in the inventory of procedures leading to these discoveries: "I will now shut my eyes, stop my ears, and withdraw all my senses"; "I will converse with myself and scrutinize myself more deeply"; "I will cast around more carefully to see whether there may be other things within me which I have not yet noticed"; "But there was something else which I used to assert, and which through habitual belief I thought I perceived clearly, although in fact I did not do so."[11] These are steps in the search for how and what the thinking thing thinks, an exercise of consciousness designed to caress from consciousness the grounds and certainty of its being.

Critics have pointed to the resemblance between Descartes's meditations and works of religious meditation. Like the latter, Descartes's work aims to help the reader to get rid of "misleading and seductive states of the soul," but, unlike religious meditation, Descartes's exercises are not intended as guides to a spiritual discipline.[12] If, as Williams writes, Descartes seeks to give guidance in an intellectual discipline, to enlist the reader in Descartes's own progress toward truth, there is also considerable self-consciousness in the Cartesian mental exercises. The *Meditations* let us in on, and spell out, a very private sort of activ-

10. Williams, "Introductory Essay," viii, x.
11. Descartes, *Meditations*, 24–25.
12. Williams, "Introductory Essay," viii.

ity. Something within the thinker's mind is presupposed, but the thinker doesn't know what it is.

Giving guidance to the reader seems to me less pressing than the essentially solitary task of providing guidance to the thinker who is undergoing self-exploration. This is not the same thing as, say, the ancient Stoic exercise of scrupulous self-examination conducted less in the service of an ideal of self-knowledge than as a kind of ethical hygiene, a practice of self-care. And while there are obvious similarities between Descartes's highly deliberate progress through the steps of an argument toward the goal of truth and Socrates' careful articulation of all the intellectual moves that must be made in order to arrive at knowledge of the nature of love or the soul, the Cartesian meditation is significantly different from the Socratic dialogue. There is always, in that dialogue, the interlocutor-who-knows, and the articulation of the stages of an argument constitute what can seem like a pseudo-exchange in which Socrates, the masterful pedagogue, guides his disciples to the knowledge he already possesses. Descartes's conversations with himself, his self-scrutinizing, are, on the contrary, not intended to educate the self being addressed and scrutinized; rather, they aim to shed light on that self, to persuade or seduce or coerce it into fully disclosing itself. The thinking thing doubles itself in order to interrogate itself about the nature of thinking.

Perhaps the indeterminacy of the Cartesian subject (the "I" in the *sum*)—Descartes's failure, as Heidegger put it, to specify "the kind of Being which belongs to the *res cogitans*"—has to do with its being a divided subject. There is the I that is searching, and there are "the things within [him] which [the thinking thing has] not yet noticed." Descartes insisted on, even exaggerated, his solitude during the years of his quest for intellectual certainty. He writes in the *Discourse* that settling in Holland allowed him "to have as solitary and retired a life as in the remotest of deserts."[13] Such physical solitude would be appropriate to the intrinsic soli-

13. Descartes, *Discourse,* 26.

tariness of the search. The ultimate goal was the mastery of nature, but knowledge of the world might also be considered (at least as Descartes stages the preconditions for this knowledge in the *Meditations*) as an afterthought in his extraordinary adventure in self-knowledge. The "Cartesian moment" may be, as Foucault claims, the prioritizing of a knowledge of objects over "care of the self," but the pursuit of object-knowledge depends on a wholly solitary pursuit of the subject of knowledge. And this latter pursuit is just as arduous as the investigation of nature. The various steps and aspects in the process of self-questioning constitute a rigorous discipline for approaching, encircling, and finally mastering the inner grounds of thought's certainty, that about which there can be no doubt whatsoever.

The "Cartesian moment" may, then, be just as much about a radical redefinition of introspection as it is about setting up the criteria for and initiating the mind's "possession," its appropriative knowledge, of the world. It is as if an essentially transparent I included something experienced as a foreign territory, one that has been obscured, as Descartes emphasizes in the *Discourse on Method*, by centuries of false reasoning leading to doubtful conclusions. True, the Cartesian "unconscious" is, at least from our perspective, peculiarly nonpsychological. It is the ground of indubitable knowledge that has been hidden behind or below centuries of intellectual error. In this respect, it is very different from more recent searches of and by a divided mind. The criteria for establishing the absolute certainty of knowledge—and, more fundamentally, the assumption of self-transparency—are hardly what we have come to expect from attempted explorations of the unconscious. And yet the exercise of mind, the arduous self-searching meticulously traced in the *Meditations*, is close to us; the mind (which for Descartes means the being) it presupposes is very much the modern mind, one that can easily appear to be the antithesis of Cartesian intellect. In the modern period, a pattern of autonomous self-reflection links Descartes to otherwise very distinct thinkers who follow him.

I will associate Descartes's modernity with Proust and Freud. The famous episode of the *petites madeleines* occurs near the beginning of Proust's monumental novel. No sooner do the tea-soaked crumbs of the plump little cake touch Marcel's palate than he feels a shudder run through him; he stops, "intent upon the extraordinary thing that was happening to me." A pleasure that makes him indifferent to the vicissitudes of life, "its disasters innocuous, its brevity illusory," has invaded his senses, filling him with "a precious essence; or rather this essence was not in me, it was me." But what is this "me," where did it come from, how can it be seized? The next two pages give us an inventory of mental procedures intended to bring to the surface of consciousness this hidden, precious essence of self. Marcel drinks a second mouthful of tea, then a third, but "the potion is losing its magic," and in any case it's clear that "the truth I am seeking lies not in the cup but in myself." Only Marcel's mind can discover the truth hidden within it. And so he tries to make the extraordinary state reappear. Here is a partial description of his effort:

> I retrace my thoughts to the moment at which I drank the first spoonful of tea. I rediscover the same state, illuminated by no fresh light. I ask my mind to make one further effort, to bring back once more the fleeting sensation. And so that nothing may interrupt it in its course I shut out every obstacle, every extraneous idea, I stop my ears and inhibit all attention against the sounds from the next room.

Finally, the memory that accounts for the "all-powerful joy" rises from a great depth of his mind: from Marcel's cup of tea "the whole of Combray and its surroundings" spring into being and are transmuted into the literary narrative of the next section of Proust's novel.[14]

Marcel's memory is of a different order from Descartes's for-

14. Marcel Proust, *Swann's Way,* trans. C. K. Scott Moncrieff and Terence Kilmartin (New York: Vintage, 1981), 48–51.

mulation of intellectual certainty. But in both cases we are given the physical and mental details of an adventure in self-analysis, of a determined effort to reach and to make present something that, without this mental work, might remain inaccessible to consciousness. This is not an enterprise of self-vigilance intended to discover sinful inclinations within the soul (as in Christian self-examination); nor is it an exercise in self-fashioning, in the elaboration of the self as an "ethical subject of truth" (Foucault's description of Seneca's scrupulous recording, every evening, of what he has thought and done during the day). Rather, the mind has become a secret object to itself; the inventory of the most banal steps in the conduct of an excavation of this hidden mind underlines the difficulty and the strangeness of entering a territory at once native to and distant from the exploring subject. The Proustian narrator explicitly recognizes the uncanniness of this psychic doubling: "What an abyss of uncertainty, whenever the mind feels overtaken by itself; when it, the seeker, is at the same time the dark region through which it must go seeking and where all its equipment will avail it nothing."[15]

The Cartesian subject-object dualism of *res cogitans* and *res extensa* is, in the exercise of thought recorded in the *Meditations*, an internal dualism of subject-mind and object-mind. The self-questioning of the *Meditations* ends with the subject's possession of that which transforms the Cartesian thinker into the one who already knows, the author as distinct from the narrator-thinker. There is no such unified subject in Proust, no piercing through an inner opacity obviously closer to the psychoanalytic mind than to Cartesian consciousness. The attempt to penetrate the world—more particularly in Proust, to know the secrets of others—continues even after it has been recognized as the displaced repetition of a hopeless attempt to penetrate the self. Once Marcel's jealousy has been unleashed by Albertine's revelation of her friendship with the lesbian Mlle. Vinteuil, Marcel makes her a

15. Ibid., 49.

virtual prisoner in his parents' apartment while explicitly recognizing that the Albertine who has suddenly become the object of a doomed need to know is actually not outside of him but within him. What Marcel calls the "inconceivable truth" of Albertine's desires is a projection of the inconceivability of Marcel's desires. Albertine's consciousness is a screen for the otherness hidden within Marcel's consciousness. "As there is no knowledge," the narrator writes, "one might almost say that there is no jealousy, save of oneself."[16] The world seen as differential otherness is a misrecognition of the subject's perception of a differential otherness within the subject's self.

The Proustian narrator's awed recognition of a vast unknown region at once identical to and other than the subject who seeks that region strikes a note that is clearly more Freudian than Cartesian. It is as if, in removing himself from all human company in order to become modernity's master athlete of self-exploration, Descartes intuited the reality of a divided self articulated two and a half centuries later as the psychoanalytic distinction between consciousness and an unconscious that is anything but certainty of being or of knowledge. In several letters to Wilhelm Fliess, especially during the fall of 1897, Freud speaks of his own self-analysis. He is exhausted from self-observation, at times dejected, but he is also exhilarated by the discoveries he is making. "Since I have been studying the unconscious," Freud writes, "I have become so interesting to myself." Self-analysis is his "chief interest. Everything is still obscure, even the problems, but there is a comfortable feeling in it that one has only to reach into one's storerooms to take out what is needed at a particular time."[17] The results of Freud's self-analysis would, as with Descartes and Proust, be made public—shared with others especially in *The In-*

16. Marcel Proust, *The Captive*, in *Remembrance of Things Past*, vol. 3, trans. C. K. Scott Moncrieff and Terence Kilmartin (New York: Vintage, 1981), 392–93.

17. Sigmund Freud, *The Complete Letters of Sigmund Freud to Wilhelm Fliess 1887–1904*, trans. and ed. Jeffrey Moussaieff (Cambridge, MA: Harvard University Press, 1985), 285 and 276.

terpretation of Dreams—and even before that Freud more or less regularly sent Fliess accounts of his discoveries. Analytic treatment itself would be an exchange, but psychoanalysis begins in solitude, and the inner storerooms are excavated by the solitary seeker with a resoluteness worthy of Descartes.

The aim of Descartes, Proust, and Freud in the passages I have discussed is one of knowledge, but the emphasis of all three is on introspection itself, both in its procedures and as an adventure. Foucault's "Cartesian moment," at least as it is embodied in these three great figures of what might broadly be called modernity, is one of a willed identity of knowledge and being. The condition of this identity is an extraordinarily active solitariness that is not a renunciatory or rebellious turning away from the world. In Descartes, Proust, and Freud an absolutely unique individuality is at the same time the key to a universal being: the thinking thing that is all human beings in Descartes, the shared singularity that art reveals and that is hidden behind particular personalities in Proust, and the universal mental functions obscured by the subterfuges of everyday conscious life in Freud.

Extraordinarily, this implicit reduction of the many to the one, the identity of the individuating with the universal, is articulated by Freud as a certain paradigm of sexual desire. The first of the three "Contributions to the Psychology of Love," the 1910 essay titled "A Special Type of Choice of Object Made by Men," may be considered as a *mise en abîme* of the self-analysis that is the precondition for philosophical and psychological knowledge in Descartes, Proust, and Freud, as well as for their relation with the world. Introspection is enacted here as a folding in of desire onto the self. The type of object-choice described by Freud in this essay characterizes a certain form of neurotic behavior, but as Freud claims here and elsewhere, the so-called abnormal behavior of the neurotics who are most readily available for clinical psychoanalytic study recalls and provides insight into similar behavior "in people of average health or even in those with outstanding qualities."[18] So the type of object-choice we are about to study is, like self-analysis itself, at once exceptional and universal.

The men studied in this essay need, as the first condition of love, "an injured third party"; they can desire only a woman to whom, as Freud puts it, "another man can claim right of possession." But the second condition in this type of object-choice doubles both the subject and the object of the injury. The loved woman must be "in some way or other of bad repute sexually": her own sexual interests have to extend beyond her husband, who is now "injured" not only by the original desiring subject but also by the other men the woman turns to. Inevitably, this makes of the lover we are studying the object as well as the agent of injury. Indeed, the jealousy necessary, as Freud emphasizes, in this sort of object-choice is directed toward all these others and not toward "the lawful possessor of the loved one." Both the lover and the husband are now together on the side of the injured. Not only is it necessary for the woman to multiply the objects of her desire; the lover himself, Freud goes on to say, repeats this kind of passionate attachment "with the same peculiarities . . . again and again." Indeed, "the love-objects may replace one another so frequently that a long series of them is formed" (*STC*, 166–68). The choice of object is a choice of objects, an exercise in infidelity on the part of the lover and the loved one; the woman may be unfaithful with many lovers simultaneously, while the man may have several passionate attachments successively, one after the other.

This is quite a cast of characters: the lover, the loved one, her husband, all the other women the lover loves in exactly the same way, all the other men toward whom the woman may direct her desire. But when Freud turns to the psychological explanation for

18. Sigmund Freud, "A Special Type of Choice of Object Made by Men" (1910), in *The Standard Edition of the Complete Psychological Works of Sigmund Freud*, 24 vols., trans. and ed. James Strachey (London: Hogarth, 1953–1974), 11:165. Hereafter abbreviated *STC*.

this type of object-choice, the cast suddenly shrinks to three. Multiple objects of desire are merely illusory objects of desire, and Freud's interpretation of the kind of object-choice he is studying in this essay will save it from the multiple traits by which its unity as a single type is threatened (traits such as the need that the loved woman desire many real or virtual lovers, the absence of any jealousy on the lover's part toward the "official" object of the woman's desire, her husband, the idealizing of the very "lightness" that sexually discredits the woman, and finally—a trait I have not yet mentioned—the lover's need to rescue the woman from the sexual unreliability that had been a principal condition of the man's desire). Freud, while recognizing the remoteness of any hope of tracing all these characteristics back to a single source, nevertheless promises that "psycho-analytic exploration into the life-histories of men of this type" will easily accomplish this task (*STC*, 168). It will, we might say, rescue the piece from its menacing confusions, and if the essay is principally remembered for the passages on rescuing, this may be less because a fantasy of sexual and moral rescue is one of the traits of this type of object-choice than it is because the essay itself is an exercise in intellectual self-rescuing.

Not surprisingly, these peculiar conditions and "this very singular way of behavior in love . . . are derived from the infantile fixation of tender feelings on the mother, and represent one of the consequences of that fixation." All the women desired in this type of object love are "mother-surrogates"; the unconscious desire for some irreplaceable thing "frequently appears as broken up into an endless series: endless for the reason that every surrogate nevertheless fails to provide the desired satisfaction" (*STC*, 168–69). We are reminded of Freud's famous declaration in *Three Essays on the Theory of Sexuality*, "The finding of an object is in fact a re-finding of it,"[19] as well, perhaps, as the Lacanian dictum

19. Sigmund Freud, *Three Essays on the Theory of Sexuality*, in *The Standard Edition of the Complete Psychological Works of Sigmund Freud,* 24 vols., trans. and ed. James Strachey (London: Hogarth, 1953–1974), 7:222.

according to which the object of desire is not the cause of desire. The requirement that the woman be sexually discredited corresponds to the boy's discovery that his parents can no longer be thought of as "an exception to the universal and odious norms of sexual activity," a discovery at once painful and sexually liberating (the mother can now be desired). But the appearance of desire is also the advent of jealousy, at which point we encounter psychoanalysis's major reductive explanatory tool: the Oedipus complex.

Perhaps because of its very reductiveness, this clarification only muddles the picture even more. At first Freud identifies the "injured third party" mentioned earlier in the essay as the father (injured, presumably, by the son's claims on the mother), although two pages later the boy himself is the injured third party by virtue of the mother's infidelity to him in having sexual intercourse with the father. Strangely, there is no correlative of the Oedipal child's murderous Oedipal jealousy of his father in the type of object-love being analyzed; the woman's husband, her "lawful possessor," was never the object of the lover's jealousy. Much more strangely, the father with whom the mother is unfaithful is actually the son himself, "or more accurately . . . his own idealized personality, grown up and so raised to a level with his father" (*STC*, 171). At first glance, the Oedipus complex reduces the number of fantasy figures to three. However, with the boy's assimilation of himself to his father, we are down to two characters, and the injured third party is once again the boy, who has become one with the father. The injured third party is internal to the conjugal couple, and in engaging in sexual relations with her husband, the woman (rather seriously manhandled in this essay) is being unfaithful simultaneously to him and to her son.

It is when Freud tries to analyze the rescue fantasy that his essay gets into its most serious trouble. He begins by acknowledging the tenuous connection between the explanation he is about to give and the rescue fantasy discussed earlier. "In actual fact the rescue-motif has a meaning and history of its own, and is an independent derivative of the mother-complex, or more accurately, of the parental complex." Rescuing the loved woman from the social dangers inherent in her "unreliable" sexual temperament, or simply encouraging her to remain "in the path of virtue" seems, however, to have very little to do with the aspects of the "parental complex" Freud goes on to describe. First of all, rescue mutates into repayment. The child wishes to repay his parents for the gift of life. With the father, the fantasized repayment is defiant: in imagining that he rescues his father from some dangerous situation, he no longer owes him anything, having repaid him for all he has cost him. Rescuing the mother takes the form of giving her a child, of making one for her, "needless to say, one like himself." Although Freud insists that this departure from the original idea of rescuing is not too great and is in no way arbitrary, it has become nearly impossible to see how this can be called a rescue fantasy. Almost as an afterthought, Freud mentions that the boy's mother had by her "efforts" rescued him from the dangers to life inherent in birth; the child he gives her is, I suppose, a tribute to those efforts, although—and Freud is explicit about this—the one being saved in this fantasy is not the mother but the infant being born (both the real son and the son he makes in fantasy for his mother).

This slippage is especially significant because just before mentioning rescue from the dangers of birth, Freud had given the final, all-inclusive meaning of all the conditions, the behavior, and the psychoanalytic interpretations that are crowded into this short study of a special type of object-choice. And once this meaning is given, it is only natural that the one being saved is identical to the one who saves, since now there is no one left but the son-lover. "All his instincts, those of tenderness, gratitude, lustfulness, defiance and independence, find satisfaction in the single wish to be his own father" (*STC*, 172–73). Astonishingly, this type of object-choice, in which objects of love seemed to multiply indefinitely, realizes the *causa sui* project, that of being the origin and cause of oneself.

The mother is the vessel, the necessary but perhaps incidental instrument for this extraordinary working out of a fantasy of self-creation. Even more—and finally—in a concluding remark Freud seems almost casually to note that rescuing the father will also occasionally have "a tender meaning. . . . In such cases [it aims] at expressing the subject's wish to have his father as a son—that is, to have a son who is like his father" (*STC*, 174). Not only does the son become his own father; he can also become his father's father. This pushes further than the son's fantasy of identification with the father. The latter has become the creation of the former. In a dizzying conflation of being, the self-fathered son is also that son's father. And why not continue this multigenerational one-ness? The new son (who was the original father) can fantasize not only giving birth to himself, but also fathering his father (who originally was his son, before that son had him as his son), and there is no reason for this fantasmatic process not to continue indefinitely. The crowd of loved ones we began with (the men favored by the woman "of bad repute sexually," the successive women with whom the lover re-enacts this type of object-choice) is more than compensated for by this potential future army of one. Except for the nearly dismissible (if, obviously, indispens-able) woman through whom all these self-replicas must pass, the psychic logic of this very special type of object-choice culminates in a fantastical multiplication of sameness.

The logic of this process is not always especially logical. The fantasy requirements of the men Freud describes, as well as the interpretive connections Freud makes among the elements of this type of object-choice, obviously do not obey the rules and procedures of conscious rational thinking. There is nothing sur-prising about this, since the connections being made are mainly unconscious and, as Freud reminds us in discussing the identi-fication of the pure mother with the harlot, something that, "in the conscious, is found split into a pair of opposites often occurs in the unconscious as a unity" (*STC*, 170).

More interestingly, Freud's own interpretations and speculations throughout his work—in particular, in the metapsychological papers, as well as, most notably, *Beyond the Pleasure Principle*, which Jean Laplanche has characterized as *un texte en lambeaux*: a text in fragments, or disconnected parts—frequently have a certain incoherent connectedness that has always seemed to me central to Freud's genius.[20] I don't mean only that he must take into account the flouting of conscious logic in the moves of unconscious fantasy and of primary process thinking. More interestingly, in taking those moves into account, Freud's own interpretations remain faithful to them: his conceptual sense fails to make sense. The Freudian text frequently performs the demolishing of its own arguments.

I'm thinking especially of the fragile nature of the dualisms to which Freud always remained attached: for example, the invasion of the death drive by the pleasure principle in the very text that was meant to demonstrate that there is something "beyond the pleasure principle," and the collapsing of the central opposition between sexuality and aggressiveness, while that opposition is being elaborated, in *Civilization and Its Discontents*. There is also the tenuous nature of the differences between presumably distinct drives or psychic categories, especially between sadism and masochism, and the always threatened merging of those drives into narcissism. Language comes too late; it depends on distinctions and intervals of which the fundamental subject of psychoanalysis, as well as the psychoanalytic subject, are ignorant. The heroically impossible project of psychoanalysis is to theorize an untheorizable psyche, and the exceptional nature of the Freudian (and, I would add, Lacanian) texts in the history of psychoanalysis is that they allow unreadable pressures to infiltrate the readable, thus creating a type of readability at odds with how we have been taught to read while also accounting for that which, in the psychic structure, is anterior to all readable accounting for.

20. Jean Laplanche, "La soi-disant pulsion de mort: une pulsion sexuelle" (1995), in *Entre séduction et inspiration: l'homme* (Paris: Presses Universitaires de France, 1999), 196.

The Freudian text performs the blockages, the mergings, the in-coherence inherent in the "discipline" Freud invented.

Aware perhaps of the strangeness of the transition he is about to make, Freud writes: "With a slight change of meaning, such as is easily effected in the unconscious and is comparable to the way in which in consciousness concepts shade into one another, [the son's] rescuing his mother takes on the significance of giving her a child or making a child for her—needless to say, one like himself" (*STC*, 173). Semantic discontinuities are, then, charac-teristic of the conscious as well as the unconscious mind, a truth exemplified in the very sentence that announces it by Freud's jump from the rescuing motif to the idea of the subject's giving to the mother a child who is none other than the subject himself. How might we speculate about the pressure that has led to this particular leap of sense, that has, I think, made it necessary? The *causa sui* project turns out to be crucial to this type of object-choice, although until Freud interprets the impulse to rescue the loved one, the kind of love he has been describing seems merely to be yet another manifestation of the Oedipus complex.

But something else has been emphasized between the Oedipal "solution" and Freud's reading of the rescue fantasy, something that, it seems to me, will provide the pressure necessary for the incongruous link between rescuing the mother and giving birth to oneself through her. Freud has said that under the sway of the Oedipus complex, the boy, blocked in his desire for the mother by his sense that she is being unfaithful to him with his hated rival (the father), finds his only outlet for his thwarted desires in masturbation, masturbation accompanied by fantasies of the mother's infidelity. Masturbation also allows for revenge against the father: it is accompanied by images of the mother being un-faithful with the boy himself, a boy "idealized" as a man equal to or like the father. The "ardent masturbation" practiced in puberty (I prefer Joan Riviere's 1925 translation of *die eifrig geübte Onanie* to Alan Tyson's more sedate, even super-egoically tinged "mas-turbation assiduously practised," a later translation used in the

Standard Edition)[21] helps to fixate the fantasies that go along with it, fantasies that are realized later by the type of object-choice that has been the essay's subject.

How necessary, or inimical, is the world to knowledge? Can thought be caressed into knowledge? Is the very notion of knowledge as something we can possess grounded in an ontology of thought as appropriative—and, first of all, as self-appropriative? Is there a nonmasturbatory mode of thinking, and of writing? In asking this last question, I don't mean, absurdly, to reduce thinking and writing to masturbation. In fact, my discussion of Descartes, Proust, and Freud has if anything raised masturbation in my esteem. Descartes shutting his eyes and conversing with himself, Proust stopping his ears and shutting out all ideas extraneous to his self-concentration, Freud's attentiveness to the associations that accompany his memory of a dream, associations guiding him to the storerooms deep within his mind—all three are moving toward what we might call sublimated climaxes (the certainty of being [Descartes], the present presence of the past [Proust], and the operations of the unconscious [Freud]), but their preparations for these discoveries curiously resemble preludes to an activity of considerably less historical significance. And yet this apparently trivializing analogy may help us to see the peculiarity of what have generally been unquestioned assumptions about the nature of thought and about the relation between thinking and being.

In fantasy, as in Cartesian introspection, the world is set aside in order that the elements of its presence within the subject may be reassembled in view of a mastering of the world—in masturbatory fantasy, a mastery coterminous with the rearrangement itself, in Descartes a mastering subsequent to the solitary introspective reassemblage of the instruments of conquest. The Oe-

21. Sigmund Freud, "A Special Type of Object Choice Made by Men," trans. Joan Riviere, in Sigmund Freud, *Sexuality and the Psychology of Love*, ed. Philip Rieff (New York: Collier, 1963), 56.

dipus complex narrativizes the subject-object dualism that has been central to modern Western notions of the bonds between the subject and the world. In this myth, the father rescues the child from the world-excluding mother-child dyad, but the rescuer is also, from the very start, a threatening intruder. As such, he may color the world with the hatefulness of a being hostile to the desiring subject. The Oedipal father embodies the world as a potentially violent rival, one that must be submitted to or gotten rid of. Once this father has been disposed of, the son, as we have seen, can be born again, this time as his own father. The *causa sui* project is perhaps the foundational motive of Oedipal rivalry. That project is much more than an avatar of a family story. It is an extravagant figuration of what may be an inescapable psychic requirement: that of the autonomy of consciousness, of thought as independent of the world in which the thinking thing thinks, or at the very least as capable of appropriating and mastering that world with instruments ranging from the crudest sexual fantasies to the most refined scientific inquiries and philosophical investigations.

Other ways of being-in-the-world, of being-with-the-world, have of course been formulated. Even within the introspective, self-analytic tradition, there are indications of an epistemologically oriented, Cartesian, or subject-object relation being transformed into an exchange between the subject and the world, one in which there are accretions and modifications of being rather than appropriations of knowledge. Except for those proto-Cartesian moments when (as in the *Symposium*), Socrates "goes off . . . and stands motionless, wherever he happens to be," absorbed in his own thought; and however factitious we may find the dialectical appearances of Socratic dialogue, the knowledge Socrates pursues is always produced within a dialogue.[22] There is Platonic doctrine, but Socratic truth, more elusively and more

---

22. Plato, *Symposium*, trans. Alexander Nehamas and Paul Woodruff, in Plato, *Complete Works*, ed. John M. Cooper (Indianapolis: Hackett, 1997), 461.

originally, emerges from a continuously renewed sociability. And if psychoanalysis begins with Freud's solitary self-explorations, the clinical practice he initiated is an analytic exchange, one in which, as Adam Phillips and I have argued in our recent book *Intimacies*, the exchange itself may be more therapeutically transformative than the self-analysis. Moreover, there are counter-Cartesian moments in the history of modern philosophy that propose versions of being as mobilized and continuously modified through exchanges that collapse the subject-object dualism. I'm thinking of Spinoza's claim that nothing is separable from a universal relationality (what he calls common notions represent mobile relational compositions); of Wittgenstein's notion of the "dawning of an aspect," which could be read as a reformulation of fantasy as grounded in the perception of external reality (the real object and its relations become "echoes" of our thought; we surround an object with our fictions in a perception at once new and unchanged); and of Merleau-Ponty's insistence, especially in the section of *The Visible and the Invisible* called "The Intertwining—The Chiasm," on the adhesion, not the dualism, of the seer and the visible (the look is inscribed in, it is the "lining," of the order of being it discloses to us).

Finally, Descartes himself proposes, in spite of himself, a non-masturbatory, world-immersed mode of thinking and of writing. By making explicit to his readers the procedures of investigation I referred to at the beginning of this discussion, Descartes initiates and sustains a kind of intellectual sociability that could be thought of as superseding the solitary concentration that led to his certainties about being and the conditions of knowledge. The use of language is already and always a frictional encounter between a nonlocatable subject and a continuously articulated otherness. (The fantasy of language as separating us from authentic being exemplifies philosophical onanism.) As speaking and writing subjects, we can't help but *fail* to reach the seductive but illusory climaxes of erotic and intellectual desire. If, as Samuel Beckett never ceases to demonstrate, language never goes anywhere, it fails to go with the others we share it with; it is, to use the title of one of Beckett's writings, "company." So, having separated himself from all society, having shut his eyes, stopped his ears, withdrawn all his senses in order to converse only with himself, Descartes, simply by his impassioned confiding of all this to us, may have indefinitely postponed that unprecedented climax he mistakenly believed was so close at hand.

4 . . . .

"I CAN DREAM, CAN'T I?"

A fairly eminent colleague recently described to me his recurrent dream: Having been invited to lecture at a university in an unidentified city, he has chosen to stay at a downtown hotel a few miles from campus. The lecture has been scheduled for 4 P.M., and at about 3:45, still in his hotel room, he suddenly realizes that he has only fifteen minutes to get to the building where his academic audience has, he assumes, begun to gather. In a panic, he rushes outside and tries to hail a taxi. In some versions of the dream, there is no taxi to be had; in other versions, his cab gets stuck in heavy city traffic; in still others, the taxi runs out of gas and he must desperately search for another one. Or, in the most peculiar twist in this minor nocturnal epic of failure to reach an assigned destination, the taxi driver makes a detour into a rural area adjacent to the city, where he stops to visit his aged parents, who cordially invite my exasperated friend in for coffee and cake. In the next frame he has somehow arrived at the lecture hall, which is—perhaps the dreamwork's compensation for his harrowing journey—packed with students and faculty. But, it turns out, my friend has brought the text for the wrong lecture, and—although he is to be introduced in a few moments—another colleague offers to rush back to the hotel and bring the text for the right one. This is especially embarrassing since my friend is aware of having a reputation on the university lecture circuit for not having the lecture he is expected to give and for having to improvise, awkwardly, with none of

This chapter was previously published as "I Can Dream, Can't I?" in *Critical Inquiry* 40, no. 1 (Autumn 2013).

the verbal elegance and eloquence for which his talks had been appreciated.

In another dream, which my friend and colleague thinks of as analogous to the one just described, he is in an apartment in Rome where he often goes for research purposes for one or two months. On this day he is supposed to return to his home in Boston. He suddenly realizes that he has only one hour before his plane takes off and hasn't even begun to pack his clothes and books. Somehow he manages to get to the airport on time, but once there he has enormous difficulty finding the right check-in counter, then has to run about a mile through abandoned streets and warehouses in order to board a propeller plane that manages to rise only a few hundred feet above ground in an endless trans-European and trans-Atlantic crawl toward a never-reached home.

Since I am not my friend's analyst, I can dispense with any therapeutically oriented discussion of these nerdy academic nightmares. Interpreted affectively and in the most obvious terms, they are panic dreams about being unable to accomplish what he is frequently expected to accomplish in his professional life. We might of course also say that they manifest a desire not to do what he spends a considerable part of his life doing. Instead of pursuing such familiar interpretive lines, I will—somewhat incongruously (but incongruity will be central to what I will be arguing)—allow these oneiric narratives to initiate certain speculations about time and logic.

It is fundamental to Freud's notion of the unconscious that its logic is without a sense of time. The psychoanalytically defined unconscious exists in a timeless present. Having said that, we have no reason to be perplexed by these dreams' major anomaly: the repeated failure to carry out movements and obligations consistently undertaken by the dreamer, in his waking life, with success. The peculiarity of continuous dreams of failure during the sleep of someone who has just as consistently succeeded in doing what he fails to do in dreams is psychoanalytically intelligible as a function of the different temporal and purposive logic in waking life and in dreams. The dream is constitutively blind to the temporal anomaly (and gratuitousness) of fearing or desiring failure *after* success, that is, nonanticipatorily. Dreams know no obligation to a before-and-after logic; a timeless terror can apparently be unaffected by the reassuring satisfaction of numerous successes in time.

I want, however, to insist on something else. Let's take a more global or unitary view of mental life. I have been making these dreams intelligible by implicitly accepting how psychoanalysis paradoxically makes the mind intelligible by its account of mental *un*intelligibility. The logical absurdity of repeatedly failing where, in actuality, we repeatedly succeed—the waste, we might say, of psychic energy on an unnecessary anxiety—is resolved once we posit a split between two modes of thinking, what Freud called primary-process thinking and secondary-process thinking or, more generally, between consciousness and the unconscious. By the unconscious, I of course mean, as Freud specifies in his 1915 essay, "The Unconscious," not the mass of perceptions, thoughts, and memories that are simply absent from conscious attention at any given moment, but rather the unconscious of repressed representations, memories, or fantasies that are not allowed into consciousness.[1] The distinction, to put it in yet another way, is between what we know (or think we know), and mental contents or impulses or pulsations whose entrance into the field of conscious knowledge is strenuously, and for the most part successfully, resisted by an ego that can itself unconsciously mount the resistance. This distinction justifies, from a psychoanalytic perspective, the rejection we have become accustomed to of a coherent, single identity, of what now seems to many of us the flawed idea of a unified self. If there is a self, it is a divided self.

If, however, we momentarily suspend our confidence about what may be the human subject's constitutive dividedness, we

---

1. See Sigmund Freud, "The Unconscious" (1915), in *The Standard Edition of the Complete Psychological Works of Sigmund Freud*, trans. and ed. James Strachey, 24 vols. (London: Hogarth, 1954–1974), 14:161–215.

may have to renounce the way we account for the double syntax of mind. Let's begin by noting that there is a great deal of communication between the divisions of the divided self. Not only are there numerous occasions early in our lives of conscious material being pushed into the unconscious; contents of the latter are also constantly striving to make their way into consciousness—a passage effected, as Freud recognized, in a variety of conscious events, ranging from neurotic symptoms to all the phenomena studied in *Jokes and Their Relation to the Unconscious* (1905) and *The Psychopathology of Everyday Life* (1904).[2] There is also the reassignment in a psychoanalytic cure of unconscious representations to what have been, until the cure, floating misplaced affects. If the human subject is divided, the conscious self is at least partly constituted by more or less abrupt intrusions into conscious temporality of material that has traveled into consciousness from that mental space or depth or neural area from which, presumably, it has been divided since the primal repression of infancy. It may take a professional psychoanalytic intervention to bring our selves together, thereby moving toward the goal, never to be achieved, of definitively challenging the very foundation of a psychoanalytic view of the mind.

The divided subject is not, however, a psychoanalytic discovery—although it is in psychoanalysis that the division becomes especially difficult to close, remaining, essentially, an intractable aspect of the mind's structure. In an essay I wrote for the journal *Critical Inquiry* (chapter 3 of this book) my major examples of a pre- or non-Freudian divided subject were in the works of Descartes and Proust:[3] in Descartes, the split between the searching I of the *Meditations* and the hidden ground of intellectual certainty

2. See Sigmund Freud, *Jokes and Their Relation to the Unconscious* (1905), and *The Psychopathology of Everyday Life* (1901), in *The Standard Edition of the Complete Psychological Works of Sigmund Freud*, trans. and ed. James Strachey, 24 vols. (London: Hogarth, 1954–1974), vols. 8 and 6.

3. See Leo Bersani, "'Ardent Masturbation' (Descartes, Freud, and Others)," *Critical Inquiry* 38 (Autumn 2011): 298–329.

within the mind (an internal version—subject-mind and object-mind—of the fundamental Cartesian dualism of the thinking subject and the world, the ontological division between *res cogitans* and *res extensa*); in Proust, the split between the anxiety-ridden subject helplessly seeking to penetrate the presumed secrets of the world and of others, even while obscurely and intermittently recognizing that those secrets are an impenetrable differential otherness within himself. To the extent that this inner division can be bridged (Descartes is militantly optimistic about this), it will be, for Descartes, Proust, and Freud, through knowledge. We can, with varying degrees of success, know that inner otherness, just as, through knowledge, we can connect to the world outside the human subject.

Foucault identified "the Cartesian moment" in the history of subjectivity as a period in which knowledge took priority over "care of the self."[4] The distinction, as it was developed in Foucault's 1981–1982 seminar at the Collège de France, The Hermeneutics of the Subject, is compelling. But Foucault failed to note that neither the Cartesian moment nor the *souci de soi* ("care of the self") puts into question a more general assumption common to both: that of a difference of being between the subject and the world. Knowledge as defining our primary relation to the world depends on an opposition made most starkly explicit by the Cartesian dualism of mind and nonmind, and this opposition accounts for what Richard Rorty criticized as the primacy of epistemology in modern philosophy.[5] (Ulysse Dutoit and I have been attempting to define a different relational mode, one of exchanges and correspondences between the subject and the world, exchanges that depend on the anti-Cartesian assumption of a commonality of being among the human subject and both the human and the nonhuman world.) The presumed divided

---

4. Michel Foucault, *The Hermeneutics of the Subject: Lectures at the Collège de France, 1981–1982*, trans. Graham Burchell, ed. Frédéric Gros (New York, 2005), p. 17.

5. See Richard Rorty, *Philosophy and the Mirror of Nature* (Princeton, N.J.: Princeton University Press, 1979).

subject could be thought of as a subjectifying of the *res cogitans* and *res extensa* dualism. In the most confident exercise of what I called a masturbatory mode of thought, the Cartesian subject seeks to appropriate, principally through knowledge, both an internal and an external otherness, one that becomes, with Freud, a radically differential otherness.

I want to argue that the idea of a divided self prevents us from recognizing the syntax of an *un*divided self, a syntax that is, however, different from the logical order that characterizes a now largely discredited notion of a unified self. In the short 1910 essay "A Special Type of Choice of Object Made by Men," Freud—acknowledging a marked discrepancy between his description of the symptoms that characterize this type of object-choice and his interpretation of the symptoms—writes that there is nothing surprising about this because the connections being made are unconscious and, as we know, something that "in the conscious, is found split into a pair of opposites often occurs in the unconscious as a unity." More interestingly, he will later compare "a slight change of meaning, such as is easily effected in the unconscious . . . to the way in which in consciousness concepts shade into one another." The transition Freud has just made, however, involves much more than "a slight change of meaning"; he has interpreted his patient's fantasy of rescuing "a woman . . . of bad repute sexually," who is the object of his amorous obsessions, as a disguised repetition of the boy's fantasy of making a child for the mother he sexually desires.[6] Such semantic discontinuities— logical leaps rather than "slight change[s] of meaning"—are apparently as characteristic of the conscious as of the unconscious mind. This truth is exemplified in the very sentence that announces it by Freud's jump from the rescuing motif in the clinical case to the idea of the son giving to the mother a child who, as Freud claims, is also none other than the subject himself.

6. Freud, "A Special Type of Choice of Object Made by Men" (1910), in *The Standard Edition of the Complete Psychological Works of Sigmund Freud*, trans. and ed. James Strachey, 24 vols. (London: Hogarth, 1954–1974), 11:170, 173, 166.

How does the inner other operate within the syntax of conscious thought? There are numerous examples in Freud of another connective logic that implicitly negates the rational dualistic logic to which Freud clings even while he undoes it. I have spoken elsewhere of the invasion of the death drive by the pleasure principle within the very text meant to demonstrate what is "beyond the pleasure principle," as well as Freud's collapse of the central opposition between sexuality and aggressiveness in *Civilization and Its Discontents* (1930), even while he elaborates on their distinction.[7] There is also the tenuous nature of the differences between presumably distinct drives or psychic categories, especially between sadism and masochism, and the further, always threatened, merging of those drives into narcissism. Such "events" in the Freudian text shatter the distinctness of linguistic categories. They train us to assimilate the principle of noncontradiction into the syntax of conscious thought; no longer sequestered within the special, "other" domain of primary-process thinking, they act along with the processes of secondary-process thinking. We should not think of the Freudian text as being at odds with itself. Its exceptional nature is to enact a oneness of being—not a divided being—which may be the most profound discovery of psychoanalysis.

A distinctive trait of that oneness is incongruity, which, as Dutoit and I have argued, is central to the structural logic of Jean-Luc Godard's 1982 film *Passion*.[8] Godard compels us to rethink an important category of thought: that of alikeness. The notion of one thing being like another is fundamental to our presumed knowledge of the world. There are several pairings in *Passion* that deceptively encourage us to look for the attribute that two disparate terms have in common. The film begins with images of traces made in the sky by a passing plane. Toward the end, just

7. See Leo Bersani, *The Freudian Body* (New York: Columbia University Press, 1986), especially chapters 1 and 3.

8. See Leo Bersani, "The Will to Know," in Leo Bersani, *"Is the Rectum a Grave?" and Other Essays* (Chicago: University of Chicago Press, 2010), 163–67.

as the film director, Jerzy, is about to sexually penetrate Isabelle, the factory worker played by Isabelle Huppert, from behind, she acquiesces, saying: "Yes, there mustn't be any traces." The remark is particularly fraught in that it extends into another implied similitude: that between Isabelle and the Virgin Mary. The sex scene begins with Isabelle's recitation of the *Agnus dei* and alternates with a *tableau vivant* (part of the film Jerzy is directing) of El Greco's *The Assumption of the Virgin*. A somewhat perplexing remark about sexual positioning is juxtaposed with a prayer and a famous painting and recalls the entirely different traces seen as the film opens, creating a connection between the opening material traces and, much later, the evocation of a humanly traceless birth. Is there a point of comparison? Almost as incongruously, Isabelle asks twice, early in the film, "Why have you abandoned me?" The first time she is sitting alone, working in the factory; the second time, running alongside Jerzy's slowly moving car. Within the film's narrative, the question is about Jerzy's intermittent and uncertain interest in her; however, we can't help but think of the infinitely more momentous version of that question asked by Christ on the cross (at least as reported by Mark) in a moment of apparent despair at having been abandoned by his Father. In each case we have an analogy without similitude or, at most, one in which the likeness between terms is faint, remote, incongruous.

Such analogies are different from both Proustian metaphors (in which two terms are presumed to have a common essence) and from more startling juxtapositions (in, for example, metaphysical poetry and much modern verse) that reveal unsuspected connective lines among feelings and objects. Whether the similitude is easily perceptible or wholly unexpected, it is presumed to be real, and we are expected to come to recognize the likeness. Such metaphors function as epistemological accretions. The singularity of Godard's similitudes is the insignificance or even the irrelevance of likeness itself to an irreducibly incongruous repetition (of two kinds of traces or two examples of abandonment) or to a comparison of terms (such as the thematic yoking together of love and work in *Passion*).

To put it schematically, it is less a question of epistemological gain than of ontological loss. The comparison of Jerzy abandoning Isabelle to God the Father abandoning his Son reveals nothing about the nature of being abandoned; rather, it trivializes the divine example of abandonment while at the same time initiating a potential likeness, one that is inexplicable and may never be made intelligible. Indeed, intelligibility is not at stake. Rather, the incongruous connection is a way of ungluing each term from its actuality. By incongruously directing them toward each other, Godard exposes what Giorgio Agamben has discussed as the potential for potentiality.[9]

Passion's narrative, what there is of it, unfolds in a frequently hectic atmosphere of people running after each other, car horns blaring into the sounds of a Beethoven sonata or Gabriel Fauré's *Requiem*, characters just avoiding being hit by a car heading straight toward them. Hectic and also comic. Or, more exactly, all this activity gives to the film a lightness consistent with the implied movement of dissimilar terms just beginning to move toward one another, thus creating a new but still undefined field of relations. It is not a question of incongruity finally being replaced by a congruity that, until Godard had put us on the path toward recognizing it, we may have failed to perceive. Incongruity institutes virtualities that have no intrinsic reason to be actualized. This retreat from the actual creates a freedom that might be defined as a kind of being to which no predicate can be attached.

To return to my colleague's dreams, we might consider his dreamt failures as having, paradoxically, a liberating effect on the actual successes. Instead of thinking of the dreams as infecting the reality with an otherwise unavowed anxiety or self-defeating desire, we might welcome them as potentializing the

9. See Giorgio Agamben, *Potentialities: Collected Essays in Philosophy*, trans. and ed. Daniel Heller-Roazen (Stanford, CA: Stanford University Press, 1999).

having-taken-place of the lectures or the trans-Atlantic flights. Having the dreams would not be the distressing reminder of a timeless anxiety corrupting the satisfaction of successful accomplishments in real time. Those accomplishments would, on the contrary, benefit from their temporal juxtaposition with accomplishment failures. In this juxtaposition, the unconscious reveals itself not as a reservoir of repressed representations and impulses that aim to block the realization of our conscious projects but, precisely because the repressive ego prevents them from being realized, as the original reservoir of psychic virtualities.

Jean Laplanche often speaks of the psychoanalytic cure not as a binding of psychic impulses that helps us to develop and solidify adaptive structures, but rather as an *un*binding of the structures that already impoverish our mental life by positing a knowable reality to which it would be desirable that we adapt. Unbinding in the analytic cure is a project of psychic freedom. The luxury of associative thinking in analysis is that of enjoying unrealized fantasies, of moving among our potentialities without the constraint or the compulsion to make them materially real. The comparatively unbound thinking in dreams is unjustly devalued if we think of it only as containing secrets about waking thought, as exposing the hidden instability of the structures of conscious, more or less rational, thinking. Rather, dreams of failures, alternating with successful accomplishments in waking life, bring a degree of uncertainty to those accomplishments, making them less definitive—in a sense, even less necessary—after the fact. Fantasmatic failures at least partially free us from the limitations of actual success; they beneficently inject doubt into those successes, successes that the dreams move into an enlarged field of potentiality. We speak of dreams as being remembered, but we might more properly say that they are permanently *present* in consciousness once they take place. They act and correspond with everything that surrounds them. Our dreams belong to the single syntax of our mental being.

For the idea of a divided subject (the psychoanalytic version of the *res cogitans/res extensa* dualism) we might substitute a notion of present consciousness as always including—processing, recategorizing—past thought and unconscious thought. The notion of memory allows us to sequester the past *in* the past, whereas remembering as a function of the oneness of being is always a project of present conscious thinking, a temporal thrusting forward. To argue for an ontological difference between consciousness and the world, as well as for a divided self (divided both between consciousness and the unconscious and between past and present) is to nourish the illusion of consciousness as a site of control. As suggested earlier, the divided self would seem to defeat the prideful confidence in a unified subject always identical to itself. But the notion of that subject as only fitfully bruised by an internal otherness intrinsically foreign to the mind in which it has been lodged keeps the otherness at a distance even at those moments when it most conspicuously disorients conscious thought. That distance objectifies the world, the unconscious, and the past, thereby fulfilling, we like to think, the precondition of appropriative knowledge. Much more difficult to master is an otherness inherent in the same, in the self-identical. In the *Phenomenology of Spirit*, Hegel writes that thinking has its otherness within itself.[10] This proposal might be taken as pointing to an ontology of the virtual. The inherent otherness of thought to itself is what prevents it from being fully realized. Thought differs before it can *be*.

It is difficult to collapse the distances over which knowledge exercises its illusory mastery of otherness. In particular, the persistence of records, of a textual or documentary past, serves the belief in the reality of the past as a kind of distinct, bounded, knowable object. Or perhaps, even more consequentially, the persistence of the past as a retrievable text means that the illusion—the hope and the fear—of a real past can't stop haunting

---

10. See G. W. F. Hegel, *Phenomenology of Spirit,* trans. A.V. Miller (New York: Oxford University Press, 1977), 34.

the virtual past, as if the notion of virtual being itself were nothing but a virtuality buried within realized being, an illusory potential for potentiality. Ultimately, there may be something undecidable about the status of what I have been describing as the incongruities of intrinsically unfinished, virtual being. How real is virtual being? And does the very ability to ask that question manifest an irreconcilable imbalance between the categories of reality and virtuality? To ask about the ontological status of the virtual is to risk having virtuality disappear into the question designed to establish its "reality." Our mobility within the evolving oneness of our virtual being does not depend on an immobilizing knowledge of virtuality. And this perhaps also means that the notion of undivided yet permanently fragmented being is a utopic notion. We can, and should, will ourselves to be less than what we are; an expansive diminishing of being is the activity of a psychic utopia.

The neurobiologist Gerald Edelman speaks of the brain as continuously recategorizing, or reprocessing, its past.[11] The past, never really lost, is, as Freud said in a letter to Wilhelm Fliess, subject to multiple retranscriptions; it is present several times over.[12] The past does not persist in the form of unchanged foreign objects buried within the psyche; rather, we might think of mental time as a spiraling movement rather than a linear trajectory that leaves its past behind. We spiral forward in time, which means that moving forward is indistinguishable from a relooping movement backward. Our futures are relooped, spiraling pasts.[13]

11. See Gerald M. Edelman, *Bright Air, Brilliant Fire: On the Matter of the Mind* (New York: Basic Books, 1992). On memory as recategorization, see also Arnold H. Modell, *Other Times, Other Realities: Toward a Theory of Psychoanalytic Treatment* (Cambridge, MA: Harvard University Press, 1996), esp. chapters 10 and 16.

12. See Freud, letter to Wilhelm Fliess, December 6, 1896, in *The Complete Letters of Sigmund Freud to Wilhelm Fliess, 1887–1904*, trans. and ed. Jeffrey Moussaieff Masson (Cambridge, MA: Harvard University Press, 1985), 207.

13. It should be clear by now that this essay is, for me, a recategorizing of some of my past thinking: a reactualizing of former work in the retranscribing context of my present emphasis on the oneness of being.

It is in psychoanalytic treatment that we may find the clearest evidence of the persistence of a continuously recategorized past in the present. And yet there has been considerable ambiguity in psychoanalytic thinking about the status of the past in mental life. In *Civilization and Its Discontents*, Freud gets into interesting trouble attempting to illustrate the affirmation that "in mental life nothing which has once been formed can perish—that everything is somehow preserved and that in suitable circumstances (when, for instance, regression goes back far enough) it can once more be brought to light." His famous analogy of the persistence of ancient Rome in modern Rome at first appears to support this straightforward declaration. A visitor will see the walls of Aurelian, as well as sections from the Servian wall, almost unchanged, and may even be able "to trace out in the plan of the city the whole course of that wall and the outline of the *Roma Quadrata*." To find ancient buildings as they were, however, is impossible, not only because "their place is now taken by ruins," but also because the ruins themselves are "of later restorations made after fires or destruction." "It is hardly necessary to remark," Freud goes on (although in fact nothing is *more* necessary to remark), "that all these remains of ancient Rome are found dovetailed into the jumble of a great metropolis [*als Einsbrengungen in das Gewirre einer Großstadt*] which has grown up in the last few centuries since the Renaissance."[14]

Freud himself practically confesses to the shakiness of the analogy when he imagines what Rome would look like if it were not a city but "a psychical entity with a similarly long and copious past—an entity, that is to say, in which nothing that has once come into existence will have passed away and all the earlier phases of development continue to exist alongside the latest one." Two examples: "Where the Coliseum now stands we could at the same time admire Nero's vanished Golden House"; and "on

14. Sigmund Freud, *Civilization and Its Discontents,* trans. and ed. James Strachey (New York: W. W. Norton, 1989), 16–18; hereafter abbreviated as *CD*.

the Piazza of the Pantheon we should find not only the Pantheon of to-day, as it was bequeathed to us by Hadrian, but, on the same site, the original edifice erected by Agrippa." Clinging to his view that our psychic past persists intact "alongside" our psychic present, Freud abandons his analogy as "an idle game" and justifies his flawed comparison by giving it the virtue of showing us "how far we are from mastering the characteristics of mental life by representing them in pictorial terms" (*CD*, 18–19).

Actually, the analogy isn't that bad. It becomes useless only to the extent that Freud holds on to his view of the mind as composed of intact historical layers. In this view, the past remains alongside a present as distinct from it as, in Freud's fanciful reconstruction of Rome, Santa Maria sopra Minerva would be from "the ancient temple over which it was built" (*CD*, 18). The view of Rome as a jumble of past and present is closer to the topographical reality of both the Italian capital and the human psyche. Having spelled out the unavoidable truth that nothing remains unchanged in the history of a city, Freud then seems compelled to acknowledge that "even in mental life" the past is preserved exactly as it was lived in the past only if the brain has remained intact and "its tissues have not been damaged by trauma or inflammation"—or, we might say more accurately, only if its tissues have not been modified by time (*CD*, 19).

Freud then turns to "what is after all a more closely related object of comparison—the body of an animal or a human being" (*CD*, 19). He then drops this analogy even more quickly, although, as in the comparison with Rome, the very unsuitability of the analogy points to the way that its original term—a mind in which nothing that has once been formed can perish—should be recategorized. While no one would claim that the body of a five-year-old boy continues to exist "alongside" that of a thirty-year-old man, it is nonetheless the case that all the earlier phases of development "have been absorbed into the later phases for which they have supplied the material" (*CD*, 19). This absorption could be thought of as analogous to the "dovetailing" of the remains of ancient Rome into the jumble of a great modern metropolis. But Freud seems reluctant to acknowledge the way in which a presumably inaccurate analogy implicitly corrects (absorbs and recategorizes) the assertion the analogy was meant to illuminate. He repeats, perhaps a bit stubbornly: "The fact remains that only in the mind is . . . a preservation of all the earlier stages alongside of the final form possible." And he concludes, perhaps a bit wistfully: "We are not in a position to represent this phenomenon in pictorial terms" (CD, 19–20). But the pictorial representation has in fact at once negated and validated the original claim.

Psychic past is absorbed into psychic present in a manner analogous to the transformed presences of ancient Rome and an infant's body in present-day Rome and an adult body. It is as if Freud realized the startling aptness of his analogies when he makes the concession that "perhaps we are going too far in this"—that is, in saying that we are unable to represent mental life in pictorial terms (CD, 20). And so he ends this section of chapter 1 with an inconclusive conclusion, one that vacillates between the conflicting views of what psychic preservation might mean, a vacillation made imperative by the very analogies intended to strengthen the original thesis of the passage:

> Perhaps we ought to content ourselves with asserting that what is past in mental life *may* be preserved and is not *necessarily* destroyed. It is always possible that even in the mind some of what is old is effaced or absorbed—whether in the normal course of things or as an exception—to such an extent that it cannot be restored or revivified by any means; or that preservation in general is dependent on certain favourable conditions. It is possible, but we know nothing about it. We can only hold fast to the fact that it is rather the rule than the exception for the past to be preserved in mental life (CD, 20).

We might have traced a similar play between opposing points of view in Freud's 1937 paper "Constructions in Analysis." There it is a question of the relation between historical truth and interpretive construction in analytic treatment. How are the patient and the analyst to determine the correctness of the analyst's construction of a piece of the patient's early history that the latter has forgotten? While recognizing the difficulty of recovering the patient's past as it was in the past, and while affirming that even constructions unrelated to historical truth can achieve "the same therapeutic result as a recaptured memory," Freud nonetheless strains throughout the essay to locate where, among all the failures to recollect exactly what has been repressed, that elusive truth, or at least a parcel of it, has been lodged (displaced or distorted) in the patient's speech and how, consequently, it can be triumphantly retrieved by the analyst.[15] Finally, with regard to the question of historical psychic truth in psychoanalysis, we should of course also mention the most celebrated example of Freud's grappling with that question: his decision in 1897 to consider patients' stories of childhood seduction as fantasies rather than recollections.

I have focused on the passage from *Civilization and Its Discontents* for two reasons. First of all, it is an instructive example of the complex operation of analogy in Freud. Realizing that the comparison with Rome is leading him astray, Freud renounces it (but, typically, doesn't erase it), concluding that psychic time can't be represented in pictorial terms. But, as we have seen, the analogy does in fact work, just not in the way Freud intended. Interestingly, though it is ostensibly abandoned, the analogy seems to have a force of its own, redirecting the argument rather than merely illustrating it. It moves the argument forward by inaccurately replicating it. For all Freud's skepticism about the usefulness of pictorial terms in descriptions of mental structure, the discussion could be thought of as an unintended demonstration of the priority of visuality over abstraction (its effectiveness is in the very passage in which that effectiveness is put into question),

15. Sigmund Freud, "Constructions in Analysis" (1937), in *The Standard Edition of the Complete Psychological Works of Sigmund Freud*, trans. and ed. James Strachey, 24 vols. (London: Hogarth, 1954–1974), 23:266.

and implicitly the inseparability of perception and theory. The former operates not merely as an auxiliary of thought; it is a mode of thinking.

Second, the passage from *Civilization and Its Discontents* enacts, in a condensed form, the relation I have been arguing for between the past and present in mental life. Freud's final position recategorizes the position he begins with. By not erasing arguments that in the course of a single text risk being seriously modified or even repudiated, Freud allows us to follow in detail that absorption of the past into the present—more exactly, that reconfigured preservation of the past in the present—that the analysand enacts in treatment. In *Civilization and Its Discontents*, the analogical repetition of the original affirmation of the past's preservation in the present at once negates and preserves that affirmation. In the analytic cure, a real, retrievable past is negated in the very process of its being reconstituted or, better, in the process of its being constituted for the first time. Indeed, the therapeutic effect is perhaps brought about by this oneness of past and present, by an erasure inherent in its preservation, by a preservation inherent in its erasure.

The type of negation that authorizes what Hegel called "the mere 'Either-or' of understanding"[16] institutes that discontinuity in mental life that leads to such notions as the divided self and the distinction between the present and a lost but intact and retrievable past. In psychoanalytic theory, repression has generally been understood as the activity separating the conscious mind from the unconscious, the erecting of a barrier constitutive of a divided subject. But repression in psychoanalytic thought is itself inseparable from the return of the repressed. What has been negated by repression is restored to consciousness, made part of the nature of consciousness. Disagreement arises (within Freud himself and in subsequent analytic theory and practice)

16. G. W. F. Hegel, *The Logic of Hegel*, trans. William Wallace (London: Oxford University Press, 1892), 180.

when the analyst, explicitly or implicitly, decides how to work with what has returned. Are symptoms, for example, to be treated as the ultimately disposable keys to the buried psychic realities they at once conceal and point to (the Kleinian inclination), or are symptoms the irreducible mental signifiers, signifying nothing beyond themselves (the Lacanian direction)? The disguises of symptom formation may be the enrichment of what is presumably being hidden, the past's absorption into a continuously becoming present.

Psychic time is not a dialectical movement from one stage to another; its mobility is a spiraling that is neither forward nor backward, and that is both forward and backward. Psychic time is unitary mobility. The very movement of thought that leads Freud to restate his original assertion as tentative ("what is past in mental life *may* be preserved") has in fact established the inescapability of the assertion. Nothing is lost in mental life. This does not mean that every thought, feeling, or impulse is always consciously realized. We could perhaps say that a mental event is virtualized once it has already been. What Hegel described as the otherness inherent in the immediacy of thought could be conceived of as a change of the ontological register. Having ceased to be, thought will ceaselessly begin to be. The present contains the virtualized future of our past.

In the 1817 *Encyclopedia* version of the *Logic*, Hegel writes: "Becoming always contains Being and Nothing in such a way, that these two are always changing into each other, and reciprocally canceling each other. Thus," he strikingly adds, "Becoming stands before us in utter restlessness." An utter but unsustainable restlessness (at least so it would seem in this passage): since Being and Nothing vanish in Becoming, "the latter must vanish also. Becoming is, as it were, a fire, which dies out in itself, when it consumes its material." This consuming fire of Becoming is, Hegel specifies, identical with Being that "*has become.*"[17] In its

---

17. Ibid., 170; emphasis in original.

inherent unfinishedness, however, the virtual never has become; rather, it can't stop becoming. The virtual is never finished with, or by, being. *It is nothing permanently in a state of becoming being.* Perhaps Freud's elaborate and changing architectures of mental life (the inner housing of conscious, preconscious, and unconscious as well as of the ego, the super-ego, and the id) was, at least implicitly, an effort to prevent the restless fire of mental time from dying out—a dying out that, however, he might have seen as continuously renewed and replenished virtuality. If a certain absent presence is integral to the evolving oneness of being, the incessant vanishing of mental events is inseparable from the multiplication of virtual connections—the proliferation of contacts within ourselves and with the world. Our unstoppable becoming is a permanent availability to being.

5 · · · · · · · ·

FAR OUT

"One of the most poetic facts I know about the universe is that essentially every atom in your body was once inside a star that exploded. Moreover, the atoms in your left hand came from a different star than did those in your right. We are all, literally, star children, and our bodies made of stardust."[1] This is a passage from *A Universe from Nothing*, a 2012 book by the cosmologist and theoretical physicist Lawrence Krauss. An anthropomorphic conceit about the stars' kindness in a similar passage from an October 2009 lecture is reformulated as mythic hyperbole when Krauss adds: "The stars died so that we may live. We don't need Jesus." This is one of many jibes at Christianity in Krauss's work, but it also struck me—to engage in some hyperbolic thinking of my own—as a reminder of the ways we can obscurely remember our origins almost 14 billion years later.

I'm not referring to the claim that our bodies are composed of the dust of exploded stars, but to the remote but still perceptible analogy between the death of stars as the earliest condition of life and a dominant religious myth of Western civilization. We are all familiar with the links between the story told by Christianity (especially in its emphasis on a virgin birth and a savior's redemptive sacrifice) and the myths of other, non-Christian cultures. I'm not interested here in the debunking potential of mythic commonalities; rather, I'm perhaps bizarrely tempted to see these myths as memories of what recent cosmological thought has

1. Lawrence M. Krauss, *A Universe from Nothing: Why There Is Something Rather Than Nothing* (New York: Atria, 2012), 17.

proposed as the origin of our universe and of life on our planet.

I'm unqualified to criticize that proposal on scientific grounds, but any nonspecialist reading or listening to Krauss might be interested in his own suggestion of the historical contingency of all cosmological theories. What we see in space and infer about the origin of the universe is a function not only of the techniques and instruments for cosmic measuring available at any particular time in the history of science but also, as Krauss explicitly says, of the position of the earth with respect to galaxies light years away, a position that varies with the passage of time. The universe is not a static object to be observed and objectively described. As the universe expands, the spatio-temporal objects of astrophysical observation change. As a result, Krauss explains, what we see today will be inaccessible to cosmologists in two trillion years: the light from galaxies we can now observe, unable to make any progress against the accelerating expansion of space, will be unable to reach us, and the four billion galaxies currently inhabiting our visible universe will have disappeared. Obviously, for that future civilization the Christian story, were it to survive that long, could hardly be thought of as indicating neural traces of our origins. Krauss emphasizes this historical variability, but, like other physicists, he also insists on our incredible luck: we happen to be observing cosmic distances at a moment when cosmic distances allow us to theorize the "truth" about cosmic origins. As Krauss and one of his colleagues puts it: "We live at a very special time, . . . the only time when we can observationally verify that we live at a very special time."[2]

For all the caveats we may have regarding current certainties about the relation between living organisms and fallen stars, and despite all the differences between religious myths and cosmological theory (most notably, as far as we know, there was no redemptive intention in the explosions of those originary stars,

2. Quoted by Richard Dawkins in his afterword to Krauss, *Universe from Nothing*, 188.

indeed no intention at all), the religious myths, I'm speculating, do seem to be remembering the origin of life as it has been hypothesized in a theory advanced centuries after the elaborations of those myths. God falls into human form so that we may be born again, saved from *our* original fall into sin; stars die, exploding into dust that would fall and eventually form planets on which the elements of star dust would be reborn as what we call life.

This is quite extravagant from someone who has criticized Freud for his comparatively modest version of phylogenetic memory. In a discussion of the Wolf Man case in my book *Homos,* I speak of Freud's "interpretive violence" against the evidence he himself records of the secondary role of castration in the Wolf Man's childhood reading of a scene of parental sex. Nothing in the case history suggests that the four-year-old resurrected his relation to his father in the sex act as one of terror. Indeed, both at the age of four and as the presumably traumatized tiny observer of parental coitus, as well as later on when he visits his sick father in a sanatorium, Freud's patient speaks of his remarkably tender and protective feelings toward the father constructed by the analyst as a dreaded castrator. But, I write in *Homos,* no amount of evidence will deter Freud from giving the father the dubious privilege of exercising his castrating prerogative. If the child failed to read his father that way, then this case history must be simply erased and replaced by phylogenetic truth. For the Wolf Man, Freud writes, "heredity triumphed over accidental experience; in man's prehistory it was undoubtedly the father who practiced castration as a punishment and who later softened it down into circumcision."[3] Phylogenesis here conveniently confirms a theory unsupported by clinical facts. While I remain unconvinced by the phylogenetic "proof" in the Wolf Man case, I am now inclined to consider the interest in phylogenetic memory as a logical consequence of Freud's insistence, in the first chapter of *Civilization*

3. See Leo Bersani, *Homos* (Cambridge, MA: Harvard University Press, 1995), 110–11.

and Its Discontents, that in psychic life everything is preserved. When he makes this claim, Freud is thinking of the measurable psychic life of individuals, but his frequent appeals to phylogenetic memory at least implicitly invite us to extend this psychic law to prehistoric and perhaps even cosmic memory.

Freud's persistent interest in phylogenetic memory may be more significant than its applications and misapplications— significant as a theoretical reflection of neurological structures. If, as Krauss points out, every atom in our bodies was once inside stars that have exploded in the course of the history of our galaxy, the preservation of those atoms might also be described as leaving us with neural memories of our beginnings. Such memories would manifest themselves not in what would be the tautological relation between them and cosmological theories about them, but rather in such things as the analogy between the cosmological version of our origins and dominant religious myths about saviors, fallen creatures, and rebirth. Krauss uses scientific knowledge to debunk religious myths of which it may remind us, but the analogy between the two could also be thought of as validating not the truth of the myths, but rather their status as admittedly aberrant memories of cosmic origins. We don't remember the origins directly, but some of our thinking derives from the neural traces that have preserved them, and these derivations are what, with some speculative license, I am calling memories.

The story of Jesus and the fate of stardust from millions of years ago: the analogy could hardly be more incongruous. Perhaps its value lies in its incongruity. As Krauss none too subtly suggests, we may no longer need Jesus, although the cosmologist's witty dismissal of the Christian story does in itself initiate an analogy between that story and the theory of stellar explosions as the precondition of planetary formation and life. The analogy does not give a new kind of truth to the myth of a god dying for the human race, but it does try out a new relational possibility: one of a correspondence between the human imagination and the history of atoms. To put this in a schematic sequence: there is first of all the cosmological discovery; then there is the perception of an analogy between that discovery and a recurrent religious myth; finally—and this is what I want to emphasize—there is, or I think there should be, an awareness of our having engaged in an unusual connective logic.

I first expressed my interest in incongruous pairings in a discussion a few years ago of Jean-Luc Godard's 1982 film *Passion*.[4] Godard casually shatters the grounds on which we are accustomed to granting epistemological authority for analogic thinking. The film affirms several incongruous couplings that are at once shocking and comical: for example, between the gestures of work and the gestures of love, between a woman feeling abandoned by a man and Christ on the cross asking his Father why he has abandoned him, and most strangely, between traces of smoke left in the sky by a passing airplane and both an act of sexual penetration that leaves no traces of semen and a miraculous birth (of Jesus) that assumes no seminal traces at all. Each element in each pairing is presumably like that with which it is paired, but—and this is what I want to reemphasize here—Godard radically revises the notion of alikeness itself.

We think of analogies as epistemologically clarifying; they help us to know the world and ourselves better by bringing together distinct units of perception and awareness in networks of similarity. Godard engages in this unifying activity, but without any epistemological gain. If we know, it is not knowledge *about* anything; rather, we know now (if that verb can still be used) a propensity of the mind to produce epistemologically useless connections. It is as if we were at the moment of similitudes just emerging—unfinished, unrealized.

To engage in this activity of positing uncertain alikeness is to expand the field of being. The relational is no longer constrained

4. See Leo Bersani, *"Is the Rectum a Grave?" and Other Essays* (Chicago: University of Chicago Press, 2010), 162–67. These pages were written in collaboration with Ulysse Dutoit. I have already given a fuller summary of our first discussion of Godard's film in chapter 4. His work, obviously, has been very important for me.

by the perhaps always illusory certitudes of similarity. In the specific case we have been looking at, the oddity lies not only in the unprovable yet possible status of a widespread religious myth as deriving from mnemonic traces of our cosmic origins, but also, and perhaps even more significantly, in the mental move that makes the connection (however lightly and in passing). The cosmological theory establishes our derivation from stellar atoms, while the analogy between a savior's death and the death of unimaginably ancient stars suggests the ease with which the human mind can, both in scientific theory and religious fable, articulate its affinity with the nonhuman. This affinity reverses Cartesian dogma: *res cogitans* corresponds ontologically with *res extensa*. Our connective field extends far beyond and before the human. We can think like matter, or perhaps more accurately, matter thinks us. To use *like* in this way invites a reformulation that dispenses with it. Alikeness is absorbed into a congruence, or community, of being.

Another way to speak, as I did a moment ago, of "similitudes just emerging—unfinished, unrealized," is to think of them as virtual. Incongruity institutes virtualities that have no intrinsic reason to be realized. Correspondences enter and leave consciousness before they can be fully formed, and this is perhaps because it is inherent in the incongruous correspondence, or the incongruous analogy, merely to begin to be. With them we can only try out different positions and extensions. The terms of our inaccurate replications, our faulty analogies, and our imperfect correspondences appear and disappear. Or rather, they are never lost, but neither can they insist long enough to become an identity that might exclude other positions and extensions. The being of the human subject is continuously intersected by nontotalizable virtual connections, all of which inhabit the same inner space, all of which contribute to the evolving and paradoxical oneness of an at once multiple and empty subject.

Cosmologists have defined the "nothing" of empty space as a boiling brew of virtual particle-fields popping in and out of existence. Krauss describes the human body in similar terms. Ninety percent of the mass of our body is nothing, or more exactly the empty space inside protons where virtual particles come and go on such a small time scale that they can't be seen. The bubbling brew of appearing and disappearing virtual particles that almost inhabit the protons of our body mass continues that activity of countless virtualities produced within cosmic space. Finally, this atomic continuity over billions of years constitutes the fundamental oneness of a universe poised from its most remote beginnings between being and nonbeing. An unimaginably mobile unfinishedness was the precondition of the original "life" of matter, and it continues to be repeatedly enacted within every living body.

I argue in the previous chapter for the importance of virtuality in the mental space of thinking. What I am now proposing is that the modalities, or perhaps even the laws of the syntax of thought correspond to conditions or laws of being immeasurably beyond and before the human. The human contains the inorganic nonhuman from which it has evolved. These cosmic correspondences are active in what we should recognize as the oneness of all being. "Should" because we also resist—most notably in the mind-body and human-nonhuman dualisms—our constitutive openness to and presence in the otherness that, from the beginning of time, has always repeated us.

.

Our real—or, more properly, our realized—identity is what we call our individuality, the particular subjectivity that constitutes us as unique persons. This is what we think of as our difference, a difference we are ready to defend ferociously, both in our individual self and in our various group selves (ethnic, racial, national, sexual). We might think of this as a psychological and moral gravitational force that pulls us away from a type of being to which we would otherwise aspire, a universal sameness to which our psychological otherness is ontologically subordinate. We fall from the richness of the virtual into the variegated poverty of experience, the experience of psychological individuality. Virtual being, intrinsically unrealized, is at once less and infinitely more than this individuality.

In Plato's *Phaedrus* (which I discuss in *Intimacies*), the recognition of a virtual being before realized individual being takes the form of a kind of self-love. We recognize ourselves in others as a type of being to which we belonged when, as immortal souls, we roamed the skies in the company of a god who embodied that type, that universal singularity. The notion of loving someone for his or her individualizing difference is an impoverished version of that love for a different sameness, described by Socrates in the *Phaedrus*. It distorts the more profound individuation of the extensibility into the world implicit in what Adam Phillips and I have called impersonal narcissism. Krauss gives us a cosmic version of this identity of being: an identity, in the cosmological story, of the matter from which we are made with the matter of exploding stars from billions of years ago. We seem never to have ceased reminding ourselves in diverse ways of that primal correspondence. The *Phaedrus* myth is one of those reminders.

The mutual self-recognition—more accurately, the recognition in the other of my impersonal selfhood—that, according to Socrates, sustains love can also be found, as Joan Copjec has recently emphasized, in medieval Islamic Sufism.[5] At the beginning of his study of the late twelfth-century Andalusian Arab mystic Ibn ʿArabi, the eminent French Iranologist Henry Corbin describes a current of thought in medieval mysticism strikingly reminiscent of Plato's *Phaedrus*. Speaking of the problem of an angelic intelligence as it is raised in medieval philosophy, Corbin summarizes the answer to this problem by the late twelfth-century Jewish thinker Abu'l-Barakat (who converted to Islam toward the end of his life). Corbin writes that Abu'l-Barakat envisaged "a plurality of separate and transcendent active Intelligences, correspond-

---

5. See Joan Copjec, "The Fate of the Image in Church History and the Modern State," in *Politica Comun: A Journal of Thought* 1, no. 2 (2012).

ing to the specific divergencies among the multitude of souls." A Being from the spiritual world accompanies a "number of souls with the same nature and affinity," souls that may remind us of all those who, in Socrates' myth, accompanied the same god in their heavenly travels as immortal spirits. In Plato, the soul in its human form seeks others who remind it of that god; for the medieval philosopher, the spiritual being adopts a more active role toward this group of souls, showing them "a special solicitude and tenderness," protecting, defending, and comforting them.[6]

Not only that: this protective angel needs the humans it protects. The most striking characteristic of Ibn 'Arabi's method of theosophic prayer, as Corbin describes it, is that it draws its inspiration from a god "whose secret is sadness, nostalgia, aspiration to know Himself in the beings who manifest his Being."[7] This is a passionate god because it is in the passionate love that his human subject feels for him that he is revealed to himself. In the Islamic Sufism best exemplified by Ibn 'Arabi, knowledge itself enters into an equation in which the very notion of being alike is preempted by a not yet realized identity of being. God's knowledge of the human subject and that subject's knowledge of him are the yearning of each one toward the other. For the subject, knowledge is loving prayer; for God, it is the desire for disclosure paradoxically realized—or rather, ceaselessly repeated, begun again—in his creature's aspiring toward him.

The Islamic mystics studied by Corbin imagine God saying, "I created creatures in order to be known by them" or, more exactly, "in order to become in them the object of my knowledge."[8] Knowledge is not something either God or humans have; it is the subject's always unfinished, always virtual activity of self-individuation, an activity exactly identical to the divine being's disclosure of himself to himself. To reach toward self-identity

---

6. Henry Corbin, *Alone with the Alone: Creative Imagination in the Sufism of Ibn 'Arabi* (Princeton, NJ: Princeton University Press, 1998), 34.

7. Ibid., 94.

8. Ibid., 114.

through a yearning for the other is the process in which a virtual oneness of universal being never stops happening. In this incessant correspondence, this back and forth of being between the human and the divine, perhaps correspondences themselves disappear, or at the least are an inadequate description of an unendingly renewed, reciprocal striving to be oneself in the Other.

.

In Proust, the concept of art as a document of the artist's authentic self is spelled out most explicitly in the theoretical discussion in the final volume of *La Recherche*. It had, however, already been explored, and in what seem to me more interesting terms, in *La Prisonnière,* in the narrator's memory of his response to Vinteuil's septet as it is played during a reception at Mme. Verdurin's organized by Charlus to advance the career of Morel, the young violinist Charlus loves.

At first, Marcel is struck by what appear to him to be the sounds of Vinteuil's individuality. What might be thought of as a certain monotony in the musician's work is the sign of his profundity. Indeed, every great artist expresses in his work what is most particular about him, his difference from everyone else: "It is to a single, personal voice that those great singers, the original musicians, always return in spite of themselves, a voice which is the living proof of the irreducible individuality of each soul." By making manifest "the intimate make-up of those worlds we call individuals," art serves "the communication of souls."[9] Does this mean that we therefore know Vinteuil, Elstir (and Proust) through their works? This appears to be exactly what the narrator means when he writes that "without art we should never know" "those worlds we call individuals" (*P*, 236). And yet the reason he gives for intimating the superiority of music to the other arts is its ontological anteriority to other "form[s] of life" that have, precisely, made knowledge (or its illusion) possible. "Music is

9. Marcel Proust, *The Prisoner,* trans. Carol Clark, vol. 5 of *In Search of Lost Time* (London: Allen Lane, 2002), 235 and 237. Hereafter abbreviated as *P*.

like a possibility which has never been developed," an intoxicating "return to the unanalyzed." The invention of "language, the forms of words, the possibility of analyzing ideas" has, it is suggested, inspired and served a powerful will to know, whereas the abandoned medium of the unanalyzed made possible (and music continues to make possible) a sharing of being distinct from a presumed knowledge of being (*P*, 237).

Intrinsically the communication of souls does not depend on a knowledge of souls. Our epistemological gains, the narrator suggests, have been our ontological losses. The individuality communicated in art appears to be devoid of personality. The narrator describes the struggle for supremacy between two motifs in the septet as a "wrestling-match of pure energies," a struggle between beings "without the encumbrance of their bodies, their outward appearances, their names." And, he adds, these impersonal energies find in him "an inward spectator—equally indifferent to names and individual character—ready to involve himself in their immaterial, dynamic combat and to follow with passion its vicissitudes of sound" *(P*, 239). What is this individuality indifferent to individual character? Curiously, the inner depth is described as if it were a call from the outside. "Each great artist seems to be the citizen of an unknown homeland which even he has forgotten," but with which he "always remains unconsciously in tune; . . . he is overcome with joy when he sings the songs of his country" (*P*, 236).

I have referred elsewhere to Gilles Deleuze's characterization of the individuality Proust finds in art as a universal region of being.[10] What Proust refers to as individual is more properly

10. See Gilles Deleuze, *Marcel Proust et les signes* (Paris: Presses Universitaires de France, 1964), especially 36–38. Translated by Richard Howard as *Proust and Signs* (Minneapolis: University of Minnesota Press, 2000). Deleuze has had a profound effect on my thought—more exactly, on the choice of the questions that preoccupy me most deeply. The connection becomes more visible, I think, in my most recent work. I'm thinking particularly of the discussion of time and of the virtual in this book (although Deleuze's presence here may be more virtual than actual). The question of the virtual struck me as important already in his *Difference and Repetition* (1968),

circumscribed by the French word *individuel*: a singular universal property distinct from the multiple particular individuals that embody it. Like the energies locked in struggle in Vinteuil's septet, the extraordinary passage we have been looking at is itself driven by a tension between the narrator's insistence on "the single, personal voice" of original musicians (Vinteuil's accent can be found only in the works of Vinteuil), and his very different suggestion that the individual in art is *im*personal and perhaps even external to the artist. More exactly, the individual in art is located at a subjective depth where, mysteriously, we "remember" a type of being that came to us originally from elsewhere, from the artist's unknown, lost homeland, which even he has forgotten and which he remembers only in his art. In that homeland, which, we are implicitly asked to believe, is the only past worth remembering, and which in Proust we can return to only in art, each of us might know again an individuality unencumbered by selfhood. That being has been obscured by the personal individuality inevitably formed by the particular history and the particular body in which our profound singularity—one that connects us to other embodiments of that singularity, to the world—has, perhaps tragically, been lodged.

To say this is to intimate that however great the gain may be, the return to our homeland (at least as Proust conceives it) can't

---

which I remember reading with enormous admiration shortly after it appeared in French. But now it seems to me that among all of Deleuze's texts it is *Bergsonism* (1966) that most closely resonates—anticipatorily and *toutes proportions gardées*—with the views of time and of virtuality developed here. (And I say this as someone who read *Bergsonism* for the first time only after completing *Thoughts and Things*!) The connection is especially evident in Deleuze's remarks that for Bergson the past is "like an ontological element, a past that is eternal and for all time, the condition of the 'passage' of every particular present," and, even more strikingly, when he writes: "The idea of a virtual coexistence of all the levels of the past . . . is thus extended to the whole of the universe. . . . Everything happens as if the universe were a tremendous Memory." Gilles Deleuze, *Bergsonism*, trans. Hugh Tomlinson and Barbara Habberjam (New York: Zone Books, 1991), 56 and 77. I am gratefully indebted to Mikko Tukhanen, who has written perceptively about my work, for pointing out correspondences with Deleuze throughout my writing career.

be made without considerable loss. The formal correspondences Ulysse Dutoit and I have studied in visual art were grounded in a study of formal similitudes between the subject and the world, as well as between subjects and between objects. In these formal correspondences, which we *perceive*, the materiality of the subject and of the world is preserved, whereas the particular accents of our being that, according to Proust, we rediscover in art, while rendering the world hospitable as a place where we can rejoin our lost homeland, can be heard only if we leave behind our psychological particularities and, it would seem, the body whose moves are in large part determined by those particularities. Our lost homeland is corporeally uninhabitable.

Might the world be the home not only of our spiritual singularity, but also of individual bodies and the desires they seek to satisfy—desires to which the world into which we have been "thrown" may frequently strike us as constitutively inhospitable? In beginning this discussion with what might seem like a fantastical fable of the body's memory of unimaginably remote stellar dust from which it descends, I meant to emphasize the material inscriptions in our body of a universe to which we belong, which we *are* before being born into it. The correspondences that most profoundly situate us outside ourselves are, perceived or unperceived, material correspondences. Living bodies do not unaccountably inhabit an alien space; they carry the memory of the origin they share with all material being. How might we be shocked into recognizing this?

What does Freud mean by a drive (*Trieb*, translated, inappropriately, in the Standard Edition of Freud's work, as "instinct")? Freud's 1915 essay "[Drives] and Their Vicissitudes" begins with a troubled effort to answer that question. A drive is not, apparently, one of those "clear and sharply defined basic concepts" that people wrongly assume to be the foundation of all scientific activity. Science begins, Freud writes, with the description of phenomena, which it then proceeds to group, clarify, and correlate. However, even at this early stage of scientific investigation, "certain abstract ideas . . . derived from somewhere or other but certainly not from the new observations alone" are necessarily applied to the material being described, ideas "which will later become the basic concepts of the science." These ideas are at first uncertain; "there can be no question of any clear delimitation of their content." They are not deduced from the material of observation, which in fact is subject to these undefined abstract ideas that, Freud adds, "are in the nature of conventions." If they necessarily have important relations to the empirical material from which, as we have just been told, they are not deduced but which they actually seem to determine, we "seem to sense" those relations before being able to clearly recognize and demonstrate them. "More thorough investigation of the field of observation" does help us to clarify the concepts underlying the investigation; now these concepts, into which the preliminary abstract ideas have evolved, are modified by the work of observation, which helps us "to confine" the concepts in definitions. Confined yet also flexible definitions—basic concepts, erroneously thought of as the solid, a priori foundation of scientific observation—are, as science progresses, "constantly being altered in their content." A drive, Freud writes, is a still rather obscure conventional, basic concept of this kind," although, after a couple of pages of what Freud describes as a physiological approach to drives, he is compelled, as he puts it, to make a further admission. We need yet another category. "We do not merely apply certain conventions to our empirical material as basic *concepts*." In dealing with what we are now looking at as psychological phenomena, we must also make use of "a number of complicated *postulates*," the most important of which, for our present concerns, is of a biological nature, and it assigns "to the nervous system the task—speaking in general terms—of *mastering stimuli*."[11]

11. Sigmund Freud, "Instincts and Their Vicissitudes" (1915), *The Standard Edition of the Complete Psychological Works of Sigmund Freud,* trans. and ed. James Strachey, 24 vols. (London: Hogarth, 1953-74), 14:117-20 (emphasis in original). .All the subsequent quotations from this essay are on pp. 120-22.

"Basic concepts," "abstractions," "conventions," "confined definitions," "postulates"; physiology, psychology, biology. The drive as drive is much more elusive than psychic phenomena such as sadism and masochism, which will be classified as specific types of drive. There is a significant hesitation about whether or not the drive can even be called a concept and, if it can, about its conceptual stability. What is it that remains constant when its content is altered? Are we dealing primarily with a physiological or psychological concept? Interestingly, the work Freud engages in at this foundational level of definition exemplifies the work of the drive itself. His conceptual wandering is an anticipatory recapitulation of the mobility intrinsic to the drive. But in order to specify that mobility, Freud finds it necessary to postulate a more general truth, about the relation of the mind both to the body and the world. He begins by proposing the hypothesis of the drive as a species of stimulus, "a stimulus to the mind." And we should remember that not all stimuli are of "instinctual origin" (an example is a strong light striking the eye). Freud then repeats an idea recurrent in his work since the 1890s (an idea that will find its most original and extreme expression in *Beyond the Pleasure Principle*, of 1920): "The nervous system is an apparatus which has the function of getting rid of the stimuli that reach it, or of reducing them to the lowest possible level; an apparatus which, if it were feasible, would maintain itself in an altogether unstimulated condition." Unlike external stimuli that can be withdrawn from by flight, or "muscular movements," "no actions of flight avail against" the internal stimuli of drives, which "oblige the nervous system to renounce its ideal intention of keeping off stimuli, for they maintain an incessant and unavoidable afflux of stimulation." But this very inability to fulfill its "ideal intention" has had, in human evolution, a positive effect: "We may therefore well conclude that [drives] and not external stimuli are the true motive forces behind the advances that have led the nervous system, with its unlimited capacities, to its present high level of development."

We have, then, developed under the stress, and thanks to the pain, of unavoidable stimulation. We might say that the drive it-self, as Freud finally defines it, testifies to these capacities, to the mind's ability to transform a kind of attack from within the organ-ism into an exemplary (highly sophisticated and potent) instance of the human organism's oneness, of a profoundly anti-Cartesian unity of mind and the *res extensa* of body. A drive is "a concept on the frontier between the mental and the somatic, as the psychical representative of the stimuli originating from within the organ-ism and reaching the mind, as a measure of the demand made upon the mind for work in consequence of its connection with the body."

Like the world, the body interpellates the mind. The latter re-ceives what it may at first take as an attack, but to which it re-sponds as if it were receiving (to use Proust's phrase) "a strange call," one that demands work. The mind seeks a "psychical rep-resentative" that will both carry and contain inherently mobile and uncontainable somatic energies. The drive is not exactly a representation of a stimulus; rather, it stands in for it, being a kind of psychic delegate of a bodily call which faithfully replicates the energy of its corporeal constituency. Drives are our psychic bod-ies; they are the mind's energetic reformulations of the internal stimuli constantly pressing upon it. There is no flight—except death or a psychotic withdrawal from the world—from the pul-sating presence of these multiple stimuli incessantly demanding to be psychically "represented." Like the floating affects that re-main in consciousness after the representations to which they belong have been repressed, stimuli wander in consciousness in search of the images or the behavior that will be our response to them. The body shocks the mind into accounting for its intensi-ties, into providing psychic doubles of those intensities, thereby responding to multiple calls, or summonses, that it reestablish and reconfirm the oneness of body and mind.

We might think of this as analogous to the traumatic shocks of art, shocks that open other relational fields that, most conse-quentially, might reconfigure the social and the political. Such traumatic effects are perhaps most strongly felt with works in which the inherently nonviable sense of art openly manifests itself as a form of unqualified negativity. To take in the negativity of Carol's withdrawal from the world in Todd Haynes's 1995 film *Safe* (discussed here in chapter 2), for example, is to open ourselves to the traumatic potential of art. *Safe* should come to us with a destabilizing force analogous to what Freud describes as the disruptive thrust of the drive. The negativity of Haynes's film may, like the drive, shock us into a particular sort of work. This trauma is not a message; there is nothing we have to translate in it. It awakens, or brings to life, a new, necessarily empty virtuality. We don't act on unqualified negativity; nor do we take as direct calls to action Genet's praise of betrayal, Beckett's striving toward lessness, or Carol's disappearance as a person. Rather, they act on us, freeing mental spaces for possibilities that, without this traumatic expansion of consciousness, we would have been unable to imagine. Foucault summoned us to seek both new relational modes and new pleasures of the body. It is unlikely that such discoveries will be made through rational reflection. We must be shocked into otherwise inconceivable states of availability. Each "strange call" opens us to *other* connections, connections to our individual bodies and to the body of the world, forcing us to see how few connections are required for mere existence, and how many more have to be established in order to create the relational circuitry along which our as yet unimagined pleasures might move in the world.

In the theory of the drives, that circuitry is limited to the body, and Freud distinguishes between internal and external stimuli. But the mind inhabits, is connected to the world as well as to the body, and we might take the mind's response to somatic stimuli as analogous to its response to demands from the world. Flight inadequately describes the mind's reaction to stimuli from all sources of otherness, external and internal. Our receptiveness to external stimuli is of course fraught with risk, most obviously in our political lives. Nothing is easier, or more disastrous, than to meet the anxiety-provoking demands of stimuli from the world by attaching them to representations meant to liberate us immediately from their demands. Demands that might expand or extend consciousness into new relations with other subjects among whom we live are projected back to their presumed sources as threats that must be fled. The refusal of the work all stimuli demand from us can take the form of an attack on an otherness that, we fear, would destroy us. The flight from stimuli is perhaps only rarely undertaken with the goal of reaching "an altogether unstimulated condition"; our most frequent mode of flight from the world is, on the contrary, an energetic attack on others, the foreign bodies to which frighteningly pressing stimuli can be most conveniently attached.

There is no reason not to include fields of thought in the relational expansiveness I have been arguing for. The first few pages of "[Drives] and Their Vicissitudes" can serve as an example, among countless others, of Freud's energetic (at times incoherent) openness to intellectual stimuli. In them Freud appears to be searching for the methodological apparatus that will lead to the definition that they already enact and confirm. The tentative, shifting thought of these pages performs the work that responds to, that is a measure of the demand made upon the energy of the mind by virtue of the mind's connection with the body. That work is intrinsic to the drive. It is what the drive does with internal stimuli. Furthermore, in calling the drive itself a concept, Freud makes clear that the short paragraph defining the drive is not the intellectual resolution of the methodological wandering that precedes it but is rather itself constitutive—at a higher level of intensity—of the work being done by the thinking that has been moving toward it. Where—in the body?—has this particular demand come from? It is as if the drive itself were demanding its own intellectual representative. The drive is a drive-driven concept.

The body is the mind's most intimate world. It extends, both physically and ontologically, into the world that surrounds it, and into the universe inhabited by that world. The difficult and exhilarating demand made on the mind by all those worlds—the call they make to us—is not that we think about or against them, but rather that our thought be the passionately energetic delegate of the cosmic explosions, upheavals, movements, and settlings that, very late in their still unfinished history, at last gave birth to the human and nonhuman bodies in and among which we live, as well as to thought and its work.

6 . . . .

BEING AND NOTNESS

Is it possible to be a father if you don't have one? A negative answer to this question is the premise of Pierre Bergounioux's extraordinary short work of fiction, *La Casse*.[1] This fifty-page work is told from the point of view of a narrator who suffers from his father not having had a father himself. The narrator's grandfather was killed during "la guerre, la grande" (World War I), and as a result, the narrator's father, born just before the war, became "father-orphaned" (orphelin de père) before even becoming aware of having a father. The narrator formulates the question I began with in terms of being and having a son, or not being able to be and to have a son: "I suppose one can have a son only insofar as one has been a son oneself."

This problem in generational succession is spelled out in a passage notable for its meticulously convoluted logic as well as for its peculiar manner of designating the human (both characteristic of Bergounioux's writing in *La Casse*). A man is first of all a son (which, from a larger perspective, is immediately a secondary position, since to be a son presupposes a pre-existent father), and if we haven't known the secondariness of our existential firstness, we will have difficulty later with occupying the chronologically first position, that of the father—a necessity if we are to leave some space for the chronologically second position, that of the son. We need to know what it is to come after someone in order to allow someone else to come after us. Never having

1. Pierre Bergounioux, *La Casse* (Paris: Éditions Fata Morgana, 1994). Not translated into English. All translations here are mine.

experienced what it is to follow, we can't imagine being followed. To be immediately first in a line of succession is, according to the reasoning of Bergounioux's narrator (the son of an orphaned father), to think of oneself as last. A successor is inconceivable to a man without antecedents. A world at war, one that could appear to itself only "in division and conflict," the narrator writes in a later passage, had made of his father "the first, and, as a result, the last." And to be at once the first one and the last one is, inescapably, to be the only one.

So if someone else were to appear—someone not referred to as a son (which has been made impossible by a cruel and violent history), but as "a thing duly provided with the generic attributes of the species"—the father-orphan can only try to persuade the "host" of this "little bag of skin" that he has no existence at all. In order to remain the last and only one, the son who never knew a father and who consequently can't be one himself, that is, can't allow any space for the being-a-son he himself never knew, must nullify anyone claiming to occupy that space. The fatherless father needs the "continued abolition" of the would-be son-ness of a presumptuous bunch of flesh that would deny him (the orphaned father) his tragic yet passionately embraced first-ness, lastness, and oneness. The "continued abolition" requires, however, that the son exist in order to be abolished. The father's immobilized being, which would lose its privileged lastness if it could anticipate a future, depends on the son continuing to be in order to continue being pushed into not being.

His father's peace depends on something even more radical than the son's continuing to be abolished, than his sustained, lacerating submission to nullification. Beyond the pure negativizing of repeated not-being is notness itself. The narrator speaks of his having to provide a not, what he calls a *ne pas*—an erasure so absolute that there can no longer be an act, a temporalizing verb, between the *ne* and the *pas*. It is as if when the son agrees not to be, it is not even a question of negating an already inert state of simply being. It is not exactly that he is not; only notness has happened, although to say this is already to violate *ne pas*, or not.

Bergounioux's narrator suggests an analogy between his father's need for the son's continued abolition and more general social structures. Remembering the period when he tried to escape his humanness by assimilating himself to a tree (I'll return to this), the narrator praises trees for their "equality" and, especially, for the equality they accorded to him. Unlike people, trees never seek to cover themselves with gold and furs, to surround themselves with shining objects that would somehow enlarge their being and authenticate their existence. Trees "were themselves without needing my approval, that is to say an alteration in my being, its perpetuated negation." It's not only the orphaned father who needs to erase his son in order to affirm his own being; all people seek to prove their existence by denying existence to others. The nullifying of the other in a family relation is repeated in a master-slave social structure (reminiscent of the one described by Hegel), in which self-negation is the slave's acknowledgment of the master. If the family relation in *La Casse* is analogous to a larger, perhaps universal relational model, the connection between the two is not presented as derivative. The family structure is not offered as merely exemplifying a more pervasive social structure. If anything, the family relation, while obviously contingent in the sense that it is historically determined in the novel by the war that orphaned the narrator's father, seems to be the ground, or condition of possibility, of all human connectedness. Human community is perverted, or invalidated, by a break within the generational line of succession. The narrator is a stranger to the world if he is a stranger to his father. We will see in a moment how startlingly bizarre the fable of *La Casse* is, but that quality is traceable to a classical or orthodox psychoanalytic reading of the relation between paternity and sociality, a reading implicitly embraced by the novel. The son must be acknowledged—protected and loved—by the father if he is to be successfully integrated into the social.

The absence of any reference to maternity (except on the novel's last page) suggests the pre-Oedipal nature of the father-son relation in *La Casse*. Not maternal pre-Oedipality, but that love for the father significantly if for the most part cursorily referred to by Freud as preceding the ambivalent, conflict-ridden intimacy with the father fantasmatically enacted in the Oedipal stage. The latter is presocial in the sense that the boy's renunciation of his love for the mother and his submission to the Law of the father presumably allow him to break out of a dyadic family structure and open himself to larger, more diversified social structures. The pre-Oedipal has, however, already introduced the child into a complex affectivity with both male and female subjects that will be present in all social relations. The father as a pre-Oedipal object of loving identification may be more of an enabling agent in this passage into the social than he would be as an Oedipal rival. In both instances—and this is what I want to emphasize— the father is the principal agent in the child's socialization. The most radical failure in that process would be traceable to the pre-Oedipal father's failure to be both a loving subject and an object of love. The inability of Bergounioux's narrator to be socially is traceable to his father's inability to love him (to provide him with a space in which he might exist independently) as a result of the absence, in his own case, of a father who might have helped him to move generationally, to be, in time, a loved son and then a loving father.

We begin and end our discussions of thoughts and things with opposite views of orphanhood. For Bergounioux, to be father-orphaned is to be deprived of a capacity for connectedness. The first, the last, and the only one: that is the type of grandiose, impossible type of being to which we are condemned in the absence of a father. And to have as a father the ruthless victim of such an absence is to experience paternity as a project of filial anni-hilation. For the orphaned father, the generative can only be a continuously renewed notness. For all its textual strangeness, *La Casse* is a compact masterpiece of Freudian and Lacanian orthodoxy. Interestingly, a woman, Claire Denis, provided us with an impressively different perspective on the consequences of orphanhood for men. The Legionnaires from the film *Beau travail* are nation-orphans from all over the world. But their having been severed, willingly or unwillingly, from a fatherland turns out to be the precondition for relational reinventions. The Foreign Legion is a community of men who have lost community, but Claire Denis's men, compelled to reinitiate the social, choreograph themselves into new groupings not accounted for by their official duties, groupings watched with what seems to be a transfixed if perhaps also amused curiosity by the African natives, and witnessed by the surrounding sea and mountains in tableaux of solemn immobility. It is as if being fatherless were welcomed as an exhilarating opportunity to expand and renew the relational field.

Bergounioux's father-orphan would brutally abolish the relational field itself. I mentioned *La Casse*'s verbal strangeness a moment ago. The work is a document at once of great verbal mastery and of an almost impenetrably awkward linguistic designation. On the one hand, there is a stupefying specificity in the naming of objects, especially of machines and pieces of metal. Words rarely used—except, I suppose, in manuals on welding and on the range and make-up of objects that can be made from iron—abound in *La Casse*. (The title refers to a field of junk metal, metal that has been used or broken up, and that the narrator tries to return to its original shapes.) On the other hand, the text is pervaded by a radical doubt (a doubt from which, as we will see, Descartes's *Discourse on Method* once promised to free the narrator).

Existing without having been authorized to exist, forced to consent every day to his own abolition, the narrator lives, as he puts it, "stuck in a shell of flesh that was foreign to me, given the absence of any purpose that might have been assigned to it." A self always on the point of being erased, burdened with a useless, purposeless body, the orphan's son is a subjectless existence. We might say that the entire narrative should be written under the sign of the doubt that dissolves the negative declaration of the book's first sentence: "Je ne sache pas qu'il y ait un sens à la vie." It is almost always the verb in a subordinate clause that takes the subjunctive. It takes what the verb in the principal clause (which could stand on its own as a complete sentence) gives to it: a negation, an affect, a doubt. The act or state of being in the subordinate clause depends on the principal verb for its declarative status.

In the French equivalent of "I am happy that you are here" ("Je suis content que vous soyez là"), your being here is inseparable from the mood to which it is connected; it is as if your being here were lifted from its objective reality to become a function of my feelings about it. But in the case of *La Casse*'s first sentence, the subjunctive is unusual. We would expect it to be written as: "Je ne sais pas s'il y a un sens à la vie." Putting the first verb in the subjunctive (and especially since that verb is a form of "savoir," "to know") starts us out with an absolute doubt, one that is inherent in knowing itself, that doesn't depend on knowledge being absorbed into a feeling about it (as in "je suis content qu'il y ait un sens à la vie," or "je doute qu'il y ait un sens à la vie"). The second verb of the novel's first sentence is subjunctivized by this weakening of what would be the assertive negation of *je ne sais pas*. Also, if the segments of the sentence had been linked by *si* instead of *que,* the uncertainty or doubt would have been somewhat lessened by being part of *si,* which includes an alternative to the absence of sense: "I don't know whether or not there is a sense to life." The novel thus begins by suggesting that as a subject subjected to repeated notness, the narrator is constitutively unable to say "I know" or "I don't know." He can't know that he knows or doesn't know.

Constitutively in what sense? What is such a creature? It is perhaps because he doesn't know the answer to this fundamental question that he speaks of his birth as the arrival of a "thing," a "bag of flesh" possessing the general attributes of the species, or that he refers to the words he forces out of his mouth when he addresses the gypsy woman who reminds him of Picasso's *Celestina* as "indoor dogs," those one can no longer put outside. Or that he linguistically ornamentalizes the simplest statement (as a result, perhaps, of being ignorant of what passes for nominal normalcy), such as when he dresses up what might have been "on continue à croire" ("one continues to believe") as "on ne laisse pas de recevoir en sa croyance." In another passage, "the essence of our condition" is specified as "a useless and brief interlude between two eternities of nothingness." Ordinary constructions are periphrastically elaborated, or a bizarre syntax makes almost unintelligible what might easily have been the simplest sentence. "Thanks to Descartes, I knew who one is, or should be" is a "normalized" translation of "Je savais qui l'on est, devrait." In addition to the peculiar placing of "devrait," "qui l'on est" is already a somewhat off version of what, according to the *Discourse on Method*, we all are: in Descartes's Bergounioux-like formula, "thinking things."

The offness, the circumlocutions, the elaborate, often eloquent observations and descriptions (there is no dialogue), the peculiar positioning of words in a sentence: all this makes for a uniquely strange textuality—but we do have a text. The narrator's fate has estranged him from ordinary uses of thinking, as well as from ordinary modes of expression, but he can explain that fate and write the history of his attempts to escape from it. *La Casse* has two different chronologies: the succession of episodes in the narrator's life, and the partial but crucial rearrangement of those episodes in his recollection of them (which is what we are given to read). The text begins with a description of the narrator's visit to the gypsy camp where he collects pieces of scrap metal, visits that belong to the third and final stage of his lifelong attempts to escape from his continued abolition. After about ten pages, a new section (separated from the first by what appears to be the penned sketch of a large fish) starts with the work's real beginning: the birth of the narrator's father just before the war, followed by the death that orphaned him.

Unprotected and unconnected, the narrator, during the first seventeen years of his life, sought to escape from the human itself. In what may qualify as the most bizarre section of *La Casse*, the narrator speaks of his decision to seek his salvation in "the woodland kingdom" ("le royaume sylvestre"). In a wooded area outside the city, the narrator would choose a tree (preferably an alder) and lean against it until, in the fading light of evening, he felt himself being merged with the tree. Immobile, he felt the fibers of his skin and the circulation of his blood being interwoven with the sap of the tree, until even the weakened echo of the beating of his heart was about to be absorbed by the alder, and "I would be a tree. I would have a taste of its calm felicity." But at the last moment, he retreated; the "magnificent offer of the "vegetable kingdom" was refused, as he puts it, for the sake of a child's life—that is, so that his father-orphaned father might remain the first, the last, the only one. The narrator must continue to be there so his father can continue to press him not to be there, so that his contingent of "less than, of not" might be provided to "the order of things." He anticipates with horror the moment when he will no longer be able to sustain, with his own daily destruction, his father's awe-inspiring and terrible autonomy.

.

Perhaps we should think of all the oddities of Bergounioux's work—diegetic, stylistic, structural, generic—as constituting an original type of philosophical writing. *La Casse* is not a discursive argument or reflection; neither is it the sort of philosophical novel most famously exemplified by Sartre's *Nausea* (a story that dramatically illustrates, through fictional characters and events, a thesis about the nature of existence). Bergounioux's subject is disconnected being, or more exactly, being working with and against its disconnectedness. Its strangeness is the strangeness of being disconnected. But it doesn't stop at a performance of radical estrangement (as, say, Camus's *The Stranger* does). Rather, its most profound originality is to embody, in its bizarre particularities, a certain movement of thought, a thought obsessed with the possible failure or success of the human to connect with the world into which it is born.

This philosophical novelistic meditation leans on the philosopher who, perhaps more explicitly than anyone else, made of an ontological gap between mind and nonmind a fundamental concern of his work: Descartes. When the narrator is seventeen, his father sends him to boarding school. One morning, before classes have begun, he discovers a book in the school study that he excitedly reads that same day and that saves him from the despair and the temptation to flee with which he had entered the study. The book is *Discourse on Method*, Descartes's account of his "adventure," which the narrator qualifies as the most noble adventure anyone has ever lived. It not only saves the boy from the notness that he had thought of, until then, as his inescapable destiny, but more crucially, it teaches him what he must now do. Instead of taking refuge in the illusion that we can augment our being by accumulating titles and possessions that will convince others of our superiority and of their own inferiority or lessness, Descartes's lesson is profoundly egalitarian. Human being can be deduced, the narrator writes, only from the fact that we think. It is thought, and thought alone, that makes each of us identical both to our self and to all other humans; we are "together in this common thought, this communion of thought that distinguishes us from all other things." Our humanity comes from thinking and not from the "gestures, things, words similar to things" through which we seek to raise ourselves above all the other humans to whom, Descartes teaches us, we are intrinsically equal.

Exhilarated, Descartes's young reader now knows how to save himself and his father. He could of course retreat into his own certainty of not being a *ne pas*, but that would mean abandoning his father to "the tragedy of his time" that isolates him in the autonomy of a father-orphan. So the narrator will spend the next seventeen years of his life trying to teach Descartes to his father, to persuade his father to accept the truth unveiled by Descartes. But he fails. Having somehow brought his father to "the threshold of our authentic home," having nearly persuaded him that he can't be the cause of his son's absence and of his own firstness, lastness, and aloneness, the narrator is forced to recognize his father's obstinate fidelity to the "tragic hours," the violent history that has made him what he is. Having lost the son who now knows, thanks to Descartes, that as a thinking thing he can never be a continued abolition, the father retreats. Disappearing into silence and absence, he chooses the fate from which his son has apparently escaped: not to be.

La Casse is a philosophical fable, one incongruously embodied in the story of a man who, having failed to become a tree, seeks to abolish the human struggle for mastery over others by preaching the Cartesian egalitarian gospel of all humans as thinking things. The point of departure for this bizarrely conducted philosophical meditation is a master-slave social structure, a structure exemplified and exacerbated in the narrator's relation to his father. The master ultimately depends on the slave for his being; the father ceases to be when the son withdraws from their mutually sustaining and mutually annihilating relation. What seems to interest Bergounioux in that relation is that it fails to constitute a connection. Indeed, the master (the father) seeks autonomy through the slave's (the son's) abolition or notness; the ideal nonrelational goal of this relation would be, for the father, the absence of a need to connect. The son, after his discovery of Descartes, is no longer available as the object-to-be-erased that the father needs, paradoxically, in order to continuously reconfirm his own aloneness. The son's role as the one to be gotten rid of makes the resolution of his aloneness the condition of his very survival. The fundamental question posed by Bergounioux's story is this: In a psychic universe in which a man's at-homeness in the world depends on paternal love and a paternal willingness to allow access to the world, how can we be in and with the world if that love is absent? In *La Casse*, Bergounioux diagrams the radical steps an unloved son might take in order to escape from his mere thrownness into an alien space.

For the alienated consciousness of the son in Bergounioux's work, there are three steps in the relational enterprise. The manner of speaking Bergounioux invents for the son brilliantly conveys the resolute nominal precision, the elaborate verbal circling around objects he can only know about (such as his own humanness), and especially the extreme peculiarity of the points of entry through which he seeks to become part of the human and the nonhuman worlds. The first would assimilate him into "the woodland kingdom." The second would be communion with his father within the Cartesian universality of human thinking. When, at the last moment, his father retreats from an apparently imminent communion, the son is "fated to come back to things." But this time he approaches things actively; it is no longer a question of allowing himself to be passively absorbed into the substance of a living thing from another realm of being. We return to the gypsy camp visited in the first pages of *La Casse*, and it is only now that we learn the reason for these visits. To save himself from the phantomlike existence in which his father's withdrawal from the brotherhood of Cartesian universality has left him, the narrator now turns to the hardness of iron, to the pieces of scrap metal he collects from the surroundings of the gypsy camp. By breaking up, hammering, and soldering the pieces of metal he takes away from the camp, the son, with great seriousness and frantic energy, manages to reconnect to the world his father had taken away from him.

There are two stages to his work. Both are part of a general design to recover "the riches of a lost world, animals, plants, and even men in an enormous pile of junk." First, the narrator works on old and battered pieces of iron in order to discover what they were originally used for. He has to go back to the beginning, to know "what he is dealing with" in a scrap of metal before passing to the stage of finding, as he puts it, that which he vehemently desires and needs from it. For example, burrowing machinery such as plowshares that had been buried in the earth have the "oblong, tapering profile of fish." By chiseling under the oxide bed, he sees "the brilliant luster common to new metal and to silver-colored fish." The wings of birds, unlike the fish whose real underwater habitat is analogous to the depths of earth where the ruins of ploughshares had been buried, are born from iron whose first use had been the opposite of flight: they were fastened to the hooves of cattle originally used to pull carts through the fields.

By discovering what an old piece of iron was used for, the narrator can see how its use imprinted on it a form present elsewhere in the world. By his feverish work on rusty, battered remnants of human work, he makes visible a vast world of correspondences. The ways in which humans once used metal gave to it forms of life present elsewhere. His refashioning of a piece of iron in order to return it to the shape of its primitive use, to the work it was made to do, recapitulates that original shaping of the metal, but this time not to appropriate it for work, but rather in order to perceive, to "know," how it participates in the multiplicity of analogies, of correspondences in the world. And the past to which all this scrap metal belongs gives a temporal depth to the narrator's communion with variegated forms of being, including human being: "the human figure is everywhere, in the round steel-like pieces of iron sunk in concrete." It should, however, be noted that all the vestiges of an agrarian society (beams and hinges from old barns, ox hooves) consent to being reborn as man, fish, bird, animal only at the end of a bitter dispute. All this metal becomes the target of a ferociously destructive violence that was suppressed during the long period of the son's trying to coax his father into lovingly acknowledging him, and that explodes now in the narrator's furious effort to make rust-covered metal return to the shapes of its original uses and to the diversity of being evoked by those ancient shapes.

As a result of his work on pieces of iron taken from a field containing about a hundred tons of scrap metal, the narrator finds access to the world from which his father had resolutely sought to exclude him. The correspondences established in the final stage of this parable of connectedness remedy the separateness of human and vegetal life by incorporating them into the lifeless metal that the narrator hammers into becoming their vehicle, or their common home. This synthesis is, however, presented by the narrator as a substitute for the real thing. His fate is "to search in tenacious and coarse substitutes for the shadow of the lost reality." The narrator's experience of universal correspondences is mediated through metal; it is the result of his own work, but except as the observer of the results of that work, he himself is absent from the connections he makes visible. He bears witness to the circulation of forms of being of which, strangely, he remains the absent spectator.

The narrator's method has, then, consisted of a triple detour: through the path of arboreal being, the royal road of the *res cogitans*, and the innumerable simulacra embedded in the inorganic. This might be thought of as analogous to Descartes's methodical detours. We are reminded early in *La Casse* that the word *method* is derived from the Greek word for "detour." The early sections of Descartes's *Discourse* enumerate all the detours he took in order to arrive, finally, at intellectual certainty. Before his retreat he had studied, and ultimately dismissed, other philosophical pursuits of knowledge; he had traveled in other countries to test the truth-value of systems of thought and modes of living different from those he had learned close to home. Most important, the universal doubt that Descartes decides to bring to every given truth, any commonly accepted assumption of reliable knowledge, is itself a massive detour that allows him to eliminate every belief that fails the test of clarity and distinctness. It is through this detour of massive doubt that Descartes discovers that which can't be doubted. Unable to doubt that he doubts, and taking doubt as a form of thought, Descartes concludes, in a much discussed logical leap, that he exists. *Dubito* translates into "cogito, ergo sum."

For Descartes, the cogito is the ground of all subsequent knowledge of the world, of the *res extensa*. The narrator of *La Casse*, we might say, detours the cogito from its Cartesian position as the ultimate guarantee of a project of becoming "masters and possessors of nature" to the implications of its status as a universal human property. We are all thinking things, which he takes to mean that human being is transparent to all human beings. A human connectedness that makes human relationality possible is an ontological given. Possible, but by no mean inevitable. The commonality of thought in no way guarantees a peaceful coexistence of living things. Both before and since Descartes, thought has failed to unite humans in the conquest of nature. Indeed, a calculus of another's thinking, which he shares with me, helps me to plot the destruction of his otherness, an otherness not protected by his being, like me, a thinking thing.

In a sense, Descartes fares rather badly in *La Casse*. The cogito might, the narrator hoped, have resolved the lack of connection between him and his father; it might have united them in the universal transparency of thought. Instead, because of his father's resistance, it is relegated to being the second step in a dialectical movement whose synthesis, far from confirming the Cartesian dualism of mind and matter, displaces the human from mind to the fundamentally random forms forcibly extracted from inorganic matter—that is, from the *res extensa* to which Descartes opposed it. Consciousness enters into the correspondences among shapes embedded in metal and the forms of living humans only as a detached perception of those correspondences, a perception that is hardly the narrator's hoped-for acknowledgment by, and participation in, a human community.

Even more damaging, this failure is historically contingent. The narrator emphasizes the analogy (which is also a contrast) between Descartes burying himself in a room in an isolated corner of Germany, a country ravaged by war, and his father's loss of his father in another, more recent war. The narrator's father, faithful to his time, is unable to enter, or to allow his son to enter, the community of thinking things. History brutally strips the cogito from the social and ethical implications the narrator naively attributed to it. Implicit in the narrator's failed experiment is, I think, a profound skepticism about the moral power of thought, a skepticism that runs counter to any humanistic confidence in the intrinsic morality of reason. Once embarked on stage three, the narrator notes, significantly, that he remembers "having borrowed, for a time, the detour of reason." So there are not only detours on the path to reason; reason itself is a detour on a desperate journey toward human connectedness. Desperate in that its presumed power falters under the weight of a double historical contingency. There is not only the war; there is also the unquestioned assumption I discussed earlier of the necessity of the father as the vehicle of entry into the social. A certain conceptual violence in psychoanalytic thought perversely collaborates with the violence of war in order to make a mockery of the relational efficacy of thought.

Finally (a third historical contingency), there is a medium necessary for the appearance of the spatial and temporal correspondences evoked and partially enumerated in the final section of *La Casse*: metal. In the novel's last paragraph, the narrator somberly reflects on the imminent end of the age of iron, an age that, he recognizes, culminated in "the insanity and the fury of our own century and has made orphans of so many small children." What the narrator calls the imperfect, heavy instruments of the age of iron have lent themselves more palpably, more massively to the production of war machines than to the narrator's idiosyncratic and solitary coercing of metal into multiple reappearances as other forms, both animate and inanimate. He concludes with the banal yet no less portentous observation that an age of composite materials, of plastics and ceramics, is about to render obsolete the products of the age of iron. The new materials are so docile, so intimately married to the uses for which they are intended, that they resist being detoured into other uses. "It is useless to hold them, to look at them for a long time; they remain intractable, dead, disheartening."

Having renounced trying to become a tree, having failed to convince his father that their belonging to the universal community of thinking things brings them together in a way that more than compensates for his father's inability to acknowledge him as a son, the narrator ends his story of failed relationality by anticipating the loss of the medium through which he finally found a connectedness between things and living creatures. He can think of himself as responsible for and participating in that connectedness: as its artisan and its witness. In the case of new materials intractable to any form different from the one appropriate to the use for which they are intended, the second stage of their existence—the one in which they replicate forms foreign to their use—can no longer be reached. "But it doesn't matter. Time will have passed. I won't be here anymore." *La Casse* ends on this note of melancholy resignation. Will an era of peace perhaps accompanying the age of plastic permit relations not considered by Bergounioux's fable, perhaps even a time of universal acknowledgment that all men and women are related (not threateningly different from one another) by virtue of their belonging to the human community of thought? The question, unasked, remains unanswered.

Like Bergounioux's narrator, I have used the word *women* only once. In addition to the other peculiarities of *La Casse*, there is a major one I haven't mentioned until now. The connective possibilities anxiously, resolutely examined by the narrator are all motivated by the aloneness into which he has been driven by his father's need to abolish him. And that need is the result of his father having been orphaned by the war. A question never asked by the text is: Does, or did, the narrator or his father have a mother? The narrator's father is what I have called a father-orphan; but to be an orphan is to have lost both parents. Our culture has, with what can seem like a deadening frequency, been called patriarchal. Without in the least engaging in the familiar linguistic coinage of contemporary cultural discourse, Bergounioux, in *La Casse*, unflinchingly exemplifies hegemonic patriarchy. It is as if he had concluded that, given the unique importance of the father in the human passage from the family to a sociality that makes the world (and not just the parents) available for relations, even to mention the biologically necessary mother would be superfluous.

At least until the very end—the dark end—of the fable. Twice in the course of his foraging among piles of discarded metal, he comes across pieces in which the kinds of forms that would usually emerge only after long periods of strenuous combative work are already visible. Although he never figures out the use intended for the first piece (a mud-colored cylinder), the second reveals almost at once its original use and its human correspondence. It had been used as a monkey wrench. The piece, which he calls the gift of the burning sun on that summer day, captures his attention before he even steps from the walking path onto the area covered with scraps of metal. It wasn't, he writes, as if the July sun was pointing a blinding finger at it. The second life that animated this object of chrome steel becomes visible only when he picks it up. "I was blinded. I was seeing a blinding. [Je voyais un aveuglement.] In my hand, it became a maternity. At least that's what is said when a smaller thing is pressed against a bigger thing." The narrator takes the precaution of adding that maybe another word would fit just as well, since only its relative size evokes an adult, and, after all, only one adult out of every two is a woman. But these doubts hardly matter. In bending over to pick up this piece of privileged chrome steel, he has the impression of harvesting a fragment of sun.

He has kept this piece close to him; he often looks at it, although he sees it exactly as it is even with his eyes shut. Sometimes he feels the need to hold it in his hand, and, "after a moment, the metal has taken my bodily temperature. Its density, which remains perceptible, seems to come from the inside." We have moved from the forms of birds and fish to the startling claim that a piece of metal has the shape of a maternity, a word that refers to the relation between mother and child, thereby generalizing, abstracting from, and perhaps ennobling the particular mother and child whose shapes he sees, or infers, on a particular metal object. It is, then, only in this final correspondence that the parent whose presence might have made this entire experiment unnecessary appears. And the narrator's casual neglect of the mother in his statement of what constitutes orphanhood notwithstanding, she occupies a privileged if useless position in *La Casse*. She is already there, her appearance in the blinding light of the sun requires no work from the narrator, and this is the only time that his relation to the living forms evoked by a piece of iron or steel (two forms, mother and child, which are already in relation) is more than that of a witness.

The narrator enters into a profound correspondence with this form of maternity; it begins to have the warmth of his own body, and the density of the metal seems to be not a property of inorganic matter, but rather something that originates within the metal. Its final form is the culmination of a process of organic growth. The narrator connects to this process; we might say that he gives birth to it and periodically renews his fusion with it. At the end of the third stage in this unique pursuit of connectedness, the narrator leaves behind the desire for an impossible arboreal fusion in order to feel, thanks to a piece of metal, the warmth of a human connection. He loved his father—beyond measure, he told us—but he is corporeally at one with the mother.

But there, perhaps, lies the problem, and the reason why maternity has not, until the last pages, been mentioned as a mode of connection or as a point of entry into the world beyond the mother. Oneness in the world is not without spaces between the subject and the world. It is in those spaces that the subject discovers him- or herself replicated in or as otherness. The fusion intimated on the final pages of *La Casse* brings us back to a dyadic union intolerant of otherness and therefore of the world. We end with what may be a salutary reminder of invincible resistance to the invention of new relational mobilities. There is the warmth of a fusion prior to the relational itself. And there is the historically powerful Law that grounds relationality in patriarchal authorization. Built into patriarchal agency is the violence of the father, who, like the father in *La Casse*, can embody the world as irreducibly different from the subject who would enter and connect to it as a new home. Even more: the violence of paternal Law (the ruthlessness of a social super-ego) has manifested itself in our history of constantly renewed wars that, depriving sons and daughters of fathers as the narrator's father was deprived, constitute history as a succession of collective fratricides and parricides.

Or can the last page of Bergounioux's work be read beyond what it says and be seen as an invitation to think of maternal warmth not as fortifying a world-denying intimacy, but rather as spreading beyond the child and suffusing otherness not with echoes of familial violence but rather with a nonfamilial familiarity? Once this happens, the father himself might become analogous to maternity. In so doing, he would become the world's non-threatening delegate within the family, thus helping to forestall the projection of dangerous difference into the world beyond the family, and the consequent temptation to return to the ambiguous protection of the family retreat. If against all probabilities this did come to pass, much time will have gone by and, I suppose, like Bergounioux's narrator—except that in disappearing he will have escaped from a world in which matter resists being different from itself, and I will have missed a utopic reality—I will no longer be here.